Library Technology Essentials

About the Series

The **Library Technology Essentials** series helps librarians utilize today's hottest new technologies as well as ready themselves for tomorrow's. The series features titles that cover the A–Z of how to leverage the latest and most cutting-edge technologies and trends to deliver new library services.

Today's forward-thinking libraries are responding to changes in information consumption, new technological advancements, and growing user expectations by devising groundbreaking ways to remain relevant in a rapidly changing digital world. This collection of primers guides libraries along the path to innovation through step-by-step instruction. Written by the field's top experts, these handbooks serve as the ultimate gateway to the newest and most promising emerging technology trends. Filled with practical advice and projects for libraries to implement right now, these books inspire readers to start leveraging these new techniques and tools today.

About the Series Editor

Ellyssa Kroski is the Director of Information Technology at the New York Law Institute as well as an award-winning editor and author of 22 books including *Law Librarianship in the Digital Age* for which she won the AALL's 2014 Joseph L. Andrews Legal Literature Award. Her ten-book technology series, The Tech Set, won the ALA's Best Book in Library Literature Award in 2011. She is a librarian, an adjunct faculty member at Pratt Institute, and an international conference speaker. She speaks at several conferences a year, mainly about new tech trends, digital strategy, and libraries.

Titles in the Series

1. *Wearable Technology: Smart Watches to Google Glass for Libraries* by Tom Bruno
2. *MOOCs and Libraries* by Kyle K. Courtney
3. *Free Technology for Libraries* by Amy Deschenes
4. *Makerspaces in Libraries* by Theresa Willingham and Jeroen De Boer
5. *Knowledge Management for Libraries* by Valerie Forrestal
6. *WordPress for Libraries* by Chad Haefele
7. *Game It Up!: Using Gamification to Incentivize Your Library* by David Folmar
8. *Data Visualizations and Infographics* by Sarah K. C. Mauldin
9. *Mobile Social Marketing in Libraries* by Samantha C. Helmick
10. *Digital Collections and Exhibits* by Juan Denzer
11. *Using Tablets and Apps in Libraries* by Elizabeth Willse
12. *Responsive Web Design in Practice* by Jason A. Clark

WEARABLE TECHNOLOGY

Smart Watches to Google Glass for Libraries

Tom Bruno

ROWMAN & LITTLEFIELD
Lanham • Boulder • New York • London

Published by Rowman & Littlefield
A wholly owned subsidiary of The Rowman & Littlefield Publishing Group, Inc.
4501 Forbes Boulevard, Suite 200, Lanham, Maryland 20706
www.rowman.com

Unit A, Whitacre Mews, 26-34 Stannary Street, London SE11 4AB

Copyright © 2015 by Rowman & Littlefield

All rights reserved. No part of this book may be reproduced in any form or by any electronic or mechanical means, including information storage and retrieval systems, without written permission from the publisher, except by a reviewer who may quote passages in a review.

British Library Cataloguing in Publication Information Available

Library of Congress Cataloging-in-Publication Data

Bruno, Tom, 1972–
Wearable technology : smart watches to Google Glass for libraries / Tom Bruno.
pages cm. – (Library technology essentials ; 1)
Includes bibliographical references and index.
ISBN 978-1-4422-5290-5 (cloth : alk. paper) – ISBN 978-1-4422-5291-2 (pbk. : alk. paper) – ISBN 978-1-4422-5292-9 (ebook)
1. Wearable technology–Library applications. 2. Google Glass (Computer) 3. Smartwatches. I. Title.
Z678.93.W43B78 2015
004.167–dc23
2015011491

∞ ™ The paper used in this publication meets the minimum requirements of American National Standard for Information Sciences Permanence of Paper for Printed Library Materials, ANSI/NISO Z39.48-1992.

Printed in the United States of America

CONTENTS

Series Editor's Foreword — vii
Preface: A Personal History of Wearable Technology — xi
Acknowledgments — xix

1 An Introduction to Wearable Technology — 1
2 Getting Started with Wearable Technology: The Current State of Wearable Technology — 9
3 Tools and Applications — 21
4 Library Examples and Case Studies — 35
5 Step-by-Step Library Projects for Wearable Technology — 49
6 Tips and Tricks: Additional Considerations for Wearable Technology — 87
7 Future Trends: What's on the Horizon for Wearable Technology? — 99

Recommended Reading — 107
Index — 109
About the Author — 111

SERIES EDITOR'S FOREWORD

Today's library patrons are untethered and mobile in a way that they've never been before. They are able to access information not only from the mobile devices they carry such as smartphones and tablets but also from the accessories they wear. In *Wearable Technology: Smartwatches to Google Glass for Libraries*, author and wearable-tech guru Tom Bruno explains how to provide programming for these cutting-edge devices to patrons. This top-notch primer provides a comprehensive view of the wearable-technologies landscape from smartwatches to Google Glass to GoPro wearable cameras. Whether you are hoping to circulate wearable technology in your library, use Google Glass for mobile reference, create first-person videos using GoPro cameras, or add real-time translation services using Google Glass, you will find out how in this guidebook.

The idea for the Library Technology Essentials book series came about because there have been many drastic changes in information consumption, new technological advancements, and growing user expectations over the past few years to which forward-thinking libraries are responding by devising groundbreaking ways to remain relevant in a rapidly changing digital world. I saw a need for a practical set of guidebooks that libraries could use to inform themselves about how to stay on the cutting edge by implementing new programs, services, and technologies to match their patrons' expectations.

Libraries today are embracing new and emerging technologies, transforming themselves into community hubs and places of cocreation through makerspaces, developing information commons spaces, and even taking on new roles and formats, all the while searching for ways to decrease budget lines, add value, and prove the ROI (return on investment) of the library. The Library Technology Essentials series is a collection of primers to guide libraries along the path to innovation through step-by-step instruction. Written by the field's top experts, these handbooks are meant to serve as the ultimate gateway to the newest and most promising emerging technology trends. Filled with practical advice and project ideas for libraries to implement right now, these books will hopefully inspire readers to start leveraging these new techniques and tools today.

Each book follows the same format and outline, guiding the reader through the A–Z of how to leverage the latest and most cutting-edge technologies and trends to deliver new library services. The "Projects" chapters comprise the largest portion of the books, providing library initiatives that can be implemented by both beginner and advanced readers accommodating for all audiences and levels of technical expertise. These projects and programs range from the basic "How to Circulate Wearable Technology in Your Library" and "How to Host a FIRST Robotics Team at the Library" to intermediates such as "How to Create a Hands-Free Digital Exhibit Showcase with Microsoft Kinect" and the more advanced options such as "Implementing a Scalable E-Resources Management System" and "How to Gamify Library Orientation for Patrons with a Top Down Video Game." Readers of all skill levels will find something of interest in these books.

Tom Bruno, associate director for resource sharing and reserves at Yale University Library, was one of the inaugural eight thousand Google Glass Explorers and has been a pioneer of Glass adoption in libraries ever since. I knew that if anyone had the knowledge, expertise, and tech savviness to write a book on wearable technology it was Tom, who went above and beyond my expectations for this outstanding book. If you're contemplating how you can utilize wearable technology in your library, you'll want to add this title to your professional collection.

—Ellyssa Kroski
Director of Information Technology
New York Law Institute
http://www.ellyssakroski.com

SERIES EDITOR'S FOREWORD

http://ccgclibraries.com
ellyssakroski@yahoo.com

PREFACE
A Personal History of Wearable Technology

FROM THE INSTITUTE TO THE LIBRARY

It started innocently enough for me. When Google announced that it was looking for a cohort of early adopters for its shiny new Google Glass device, I answered the call with a nod back to my undergraduate years at MIT in the early 1990s, where the wearable computing project was just getting underway. I have fond memories of spotting Thad Starner (now known as the father of wearable technology), wandering around the Porter Square Star Market looking as if he'd been assimilated by the Borg, that terrifying yet strangely alluring cybernetic villain from *Star Trek: The Next Generation*. Although my education ended up taking me about as far away from computer science and electrical engineering as one could possibly go, I never stopped being enamored with technology and its convergence with everyday human life. Neither did Starner, who continued his pioneering work in the field of wearable computing, eventually becoming professor of computer engineering at Georgia Tech and the head of Project Glass at Google.

Oddly enough, I became a total Google fanboy at the same time that I'd become a librarian (or maybe this isn't so odd in retrospect, given that the digital revolution was fully underway in librarianship at the time I was finishing my library and information science [LIS] degree). One of my professors had begun her seminar by exhorting us all to create Gmail accounts, as the service had just become available to the public earlier that year; and in my final class in the program, "The Literature of the Humanities," we spent a great amount of time studying the Google book scan project—which was then in its infancy and still a year away from its first lawsuit—and what such a large-scale scanning initiative meant for our discipline, the academy, and the future of the libraries and the written word. Needless to say, as soon as I heard of Google Glass I knew I'd want to get my hands on one of the devices, so it was inevitable that I'd take part in Google's #ifihadglass competition.

IF I HAD GLASS...

The rules of the competition were quite simple: send a tweet or update on Google+ explaining why you'd make an excellent choice for helping test Google Glass and you could be chosen as one of the inaugural group of "Glass Explorers." Although Google had already reached out to developers and other tech industry pundits with early prototypes of the device to help generate positive buzz for their new product, the Glass Explorers program would select representatives from many various walks of life. Google would choose not only programmers and stereotypically tech-savvy users for its Explorer programs but also artists, educators, athletes, celebrities, and even firefighters to help them understand how a cross-section of potential future users would make use of wearable technology. This, incidentally, is one of the ways that we approached loaning our Glass devices here at Yale out to our faculty, students, and staff—our Yale Bass Glass program is as much an experimental laboratory in wearable technology as it is a project with specific aims and goals. Instead of dictating how these devices should be incorporated into teaching, learning, and research, we have asked our library patrons to experiment with the devices on their own and let us know what they find Google Glass a useful tool for in their own work; so too has been Google's approach in selecting its inaugural class of Glass Explorers.

If I had Glass, I had tweeted to Google, "I'd finally feel as cool as the wearable computing kids at MIT." It never occurred to me that I'd be selected as one of their eight thousand inaugural Glass Explorers, however. My desire to play with this new digital toy was surely as great as the other gazillion people who tweeted (or whatever the equivalent is called for Google+) their case to be included in the program, and my answer was heartfelt, but it was a little on the flip side and more than a little lacking in specificity. So when I did get the nod from Google, I was flabbergasted to say the least. Then I was saddened and somewhat deflated when I realized that, with a second child on the way, there was no way I'd be able to justify ponying up the $1,500 I'd need in order to get my very own Glass device as I had originally hoped.

BRINGING WEARABLE TECHNOLOGY TO THE LIBRARY

At first I considered using a Kickstarter to obtain the necessary funds. I was going to call it "The Glass Library," and the idea would be that each backer would be allowed to "borrow" the device for a certain amount of prorated time, to do with it as they will. The mechanics of shipping the item from borrower to borrower seemed somewhat challenging, but I certainly had enough colleagues out there in libraryland who might be willing to contribute to such a project in exchange for some quality time with Google Glass. At this point it occurred to me that other librarians might have also been chosen as Glass Explorers, so I reached out on social media to see what they were doing with their invitations. If they weren't able to purchase the device for themselves, were they finding ways to involve their libraries instead? Sure enough, a few of my colleagues responded that they'd approached their Powers That Be about funding their purchase and that one or two of them had succeeded in getting approval to buy them for their library.

This was encouraging news, as at first it seemed that the terms of service for the Glass Explorers program precluded any such institutional purchasing. Emboldened by my colleagues' success, I asked my boss, the head of Access Services, if he thought we might able to do the same for our undergraduate Bass Library, especially since it already had an ever-growing collection of circulating media equipment that could be checked out by the Yale faculty, students, and the staff. He liked the idea but suggested we bring our Instructional Technology Group (ITG) and Student Technology Collaborative (STC) on board with the purchase as well, not just to share the cost, but to widen the pool of poten-

foster a sense of innovation and experimentation among your patrons, your staff, and other stakeholders in your library community—because without the latter, it will be very difficult to sustain the former.

In this sense I'd like you to think of this book as your cheerleader, providing inspiration to make it happen. At the time of writing this book, the future of wearable technology is still uncertain, but what I hope will become clear is that libraries have a unique opportunity to help shape this future and that moreover our patrons are increasingly depending on us to fulfill that role.

ACKNOWLEDGMENTS

It isn't every day that someone asks you to write a book for them, so first and foremost I'd like to thank my editor Ellyssa Kroski—I've greatly appreciated your insights and encouragement along the way. I'm also grateful to my supervisor Brad Warren for being just crazy enough to indulge my wild scheme to bring Google Glass to the Yale University Library and set this whole project in motion. Thanks as well to the other members of the Bass Glass Project: Christopher Medeiros, Matthew Regan, and Emily Horning.

I'd be terribly remiss if I didn't acknowledge my original inspiration in the subject of wearable technology, associate professor at Georgia Institute of Technology's School of Interactive Computing Thad Starner. Seeing you walk around the MIT campus wearing "The Lizzy" in the early 1990s was one of the formative experiences of my life as a wide-eyed young futurist. I am also thankful to Jenny Levine for bringing Google Glass front and center (and on her forehead) to the American Library Association's attention and helping identify wearable technology as a subject worthy of librarians' time, effort, and enthusiasm.

Thanks as well to the many library workers whose own explorations with Google Glass and other forms of wearable technology have informed the writing of this book. It was the hardest thing in the world to try to keep up with all of you while I tried to bring this project to a successful completion, but my manuscript is all the better for it. Keep on trying new things and inspiring others to do the same.

Finally, I would like to thank my wife Maria for being there for me at every step along the way during this project, from being as thrilled as I was when I got the contract to cheering me on through these grueling last few weeks of writing and editing—this book wouldn't have happened without you, agapi mou! Thanks also to my daughter Andriana, who proudly told her middle school classmates that her daddy was a writer, and my son Mario, who only knows a few words so far but manages to inspire me with every single one of them nonetheless. To my dad, thank you for your faith in me as I've found my way. And to my mother, who always said I should be a writer: I guess you were right after all.

I

AN INTRODUCTION TO WEARABLE TECHNOLOGY

WHAT IS WEARABLE TECHNOLOGY? HISTORY OF WEARABLE TECHNOLOGY

Ancient Antecedents

Wearable technology, despite being hailed as the next big thing, has actually been around for quite some time. The earliest example of functional wearable technology dates all the way back to the Qing dynasty (seventeenth century CE) in China, in the form of a tiny abacus mounted atop a ring. Spectacles, invented in Italy around the thirteenth century CE, rapidly spread throughout Europe and beyond both as a status symbol as well as an enhancement to reading. Historians of science and technology also consider the evolution of the timepiece from large and immobile clocks to the pocketwatch and then the wristwatch an important transition from the concept of "bearable" technology to "wearable" technology.

Modern Development

The first modern examples of wearable technology were developed in the 1960s and 1970s as a way to help gamblers predict roulette and count cards in blackjack, respectively, but wearable tech had its first mainstream moment in 1975, when the Hamilton Watch Company

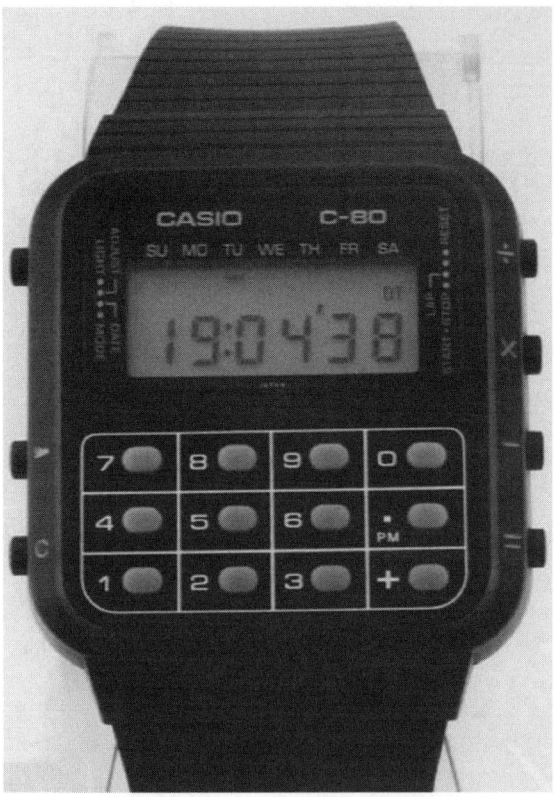

Casio C-80 watch. *Source:* "Top 15 Classic Calculator Watches: 1980 First Casio Calculator Watch C-80," OObject, 2008, http://www.oobject.com/.

introduced the digital Pulsar watch, which included a built-in calculator. By the mid-1980s, the Japanese electronics company Casio had improved upon this basic functionality, offering calculator watches that could also store appointments, names, addresses, and phone numbers in its onboard memory. Interestingly enough, the wristwatch has recently come full circle in the development of wearable technology, with Apple, Samsung, and other consumer electronics manufacturers racing to bring their competing versions of smartwatch products.

The watershed moment in the history of wearable technology, however, was the creation of the first wearable computer—a backpack-mounted 6502-based wearable multimedia computer, complete with attached video cameras—by Steve Mann in 1981. Mann, often hailed as the "father of wearable computing," went on to become a founding member of the Wearable Computing Group at MIT, whose alumni include Georgia Tech professor and Google Glass project manager Thad Starner, as well as other pioneers in the emerging field of wearable technology.

Failure to Thrive?

While wearable computing continued to evolve through the 1980s and 1990s through experimentation and development by the Wearable Computing Group and other such pioneers, commercial success eluded these groups, as the existing solutions for visual displays, user input, data storage, and battery life all continued to present formidable difficulties in making wearable-tech devices more mainstream. Battery life, for example, is still a huge problem with handheld technology and smartphones, and constitutes an even greater challenge for wearable technology—consider, for example, that the battery life for Google Glass is still only about one and a half to two hours on a full charge. The question of powering these devices has been one that has preoccupied wearable-technology developers for quite some time (for a novel solution to the problem of powering wearable technology, see Thad Starner's 1996 article "Human-powered wearable computing," in *IBM Systems Journal* 35, nos. 3 and 4).

Also, the social mores of wearable technology have proven to be an additional impediment to the mainstreaming of such devices. Even if thanks to the smartphone revolution there is significantly less bias attached to the notion of walking around with a computer in your hand or attached to your body, there is a conceptual difference between the more passive "just in case" wearable technology exemplified by the current utility of Bluetooth headsets and Fitbit bracelets, or the future similar potential of smartwatches. The idea of people walking around wearing cameras that are potentially always taking photos or recording video footage, however, evokes powerful fears surrounding issues of surveillance and individual privacy, themes we will explore at greater length later in this book.

FUTURE OF WEARABLE TECHNOLOGY: HOW SOON IS NOW?

All of these considerations notwithstanding, whether or not wearable technology will carry the day in the hearts and minds of the average consumer and in what form ultimately depends on the practical usefulness of such devices in everyday life. Consider the smartphone. How did we move so quickly from a paradigm where mobile technology was considered to be an expensive and intrusive toy for the ultrarich to one where everyone was walking around with a handheld wireless computer as their primary means of communication, navigation, and information? If the cycle from ridicule to ubiquity is anything like the mobile-telephone revolution, we are ignoring wearable technology at our own peril, but at the moment wearable tech is waiting for its breakthrough device.

Will it be Google Glass? After two years of a tightly controlled and small circle of alpha testers from among the software developer and

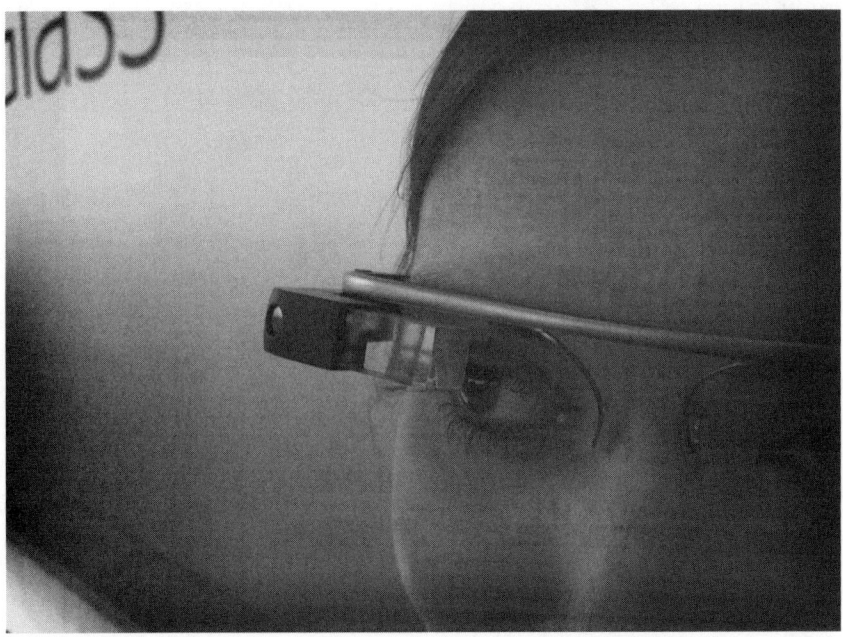

Google Glass Explorer edition. Photo by Antonio Zugaldia, Flickr.

tech journalist industries, Google opened the ranks of Glass owners first through its Glass Explorers program (where it enlisted artists, educators, and librarians, as well as other key professions that stood to benefit from innovation in the field of wearable technology) over the summer of 2013, and then by making the beta testing period open to all interested parties in spring 2014.

In January 2015, Google announced it would be ending the Glass Explorers program and discontinuing sales of its prototype device to individuals, although companies and developers working with wearable technology would still be able to purchase the device. In the meantime, Google has "graduated" its Project Glass from the experimental Google X division and placed it under the same direction as Nest Labs, which is responsible for developing smart-home technology and the Internet of Things. Unlike the relatively open alpha- and beta-testing periods during which Google relied on the public to help field-test the Glass device and mainstream the still radical concept of using conspicuous wearable technology in one's daily business, the development of the next version of Google Glass will be closed until Google feels that the device is ready for sale to the general public.

> The more secretive approach differs from Google's usual pattern. As a mainly software company, Google likes to release early versions of its products to a test group, collect their feedback and then quickly update to fix problems. That's how it rolled out Gmail in 2004.
> But that launch-and-iterate approach backfired with Glass, one of the few consumer-hardware devices the company designed and built in-house. The gadget proved more difficult to update than software code running a service like Gmail.
> Glass is part of a broader push by Google to expand from its software roots into physical devices that are connected to the Internet. But the company is still grappling with the best way to design and build hardware. (Alistair Barr, "Google Glass Gets a New Direction," *Wall Street Journal*, January 15, 2015, http://www.wsj.com/)

In the meantime, other companies have been busy trying to bring their own wearable-technology devices to market in time to compete with Glass. Especially now that Google has closed the open beta period for its Glass Explorers program and discontinued sales of the Glass prototype device, it is useful to see what Google's rivals are hoping to release in advance of a potential "Google Glass 2" launch of a nonbeta consumer edition of Glass later in 2015. As of January 2015, both Sony and Toshiba have developed wearable glasses prototypes—neither of them is available for sale yet to the general public, but Sony has already released the developers' kit to programmers, a positive sign that a commercial release will be happening soon. Also, at the most recent Computer Electronics Show, Sony debuted a clip-on version of its SmartEyeglasses prototype, called Attach! which can be mounted to any existing pair of glasses or sunglasses ("CES 2015 Coverage," Digital Trends, accessed April 10, 2015, http://www.digitaltrends.com/). It remains to be seen, however, if any of these devices will manage to capture the hearts and minds of the emerging wearable-technology consumer, or if like Google Glass, these products will continue to struggle to find a market even as other wearable-tech devices find their commercial niches and prosper.

WEARABLE TECHNOLOGY VERSUS IMMERSIVE TECHNOLOGY: IS THE FUTURE AUGMENTED, OR IS IT VIRTUAL?

An interesting development that we will also explore is the recent emergence of immersive "virtual reality" viewers such as the Oculus Rift. A field of wearable technology that quite honestly had been languishing for more than a decade has suddenly burst out into the mainstream, but what does the Rift and other forms of 3-D wearable displays mean for libraries? In this book we will examine how immersive technology is being developed in the gaming and consumer electronic industries, and take a quick inventory of libraries that are already trying to make sense of this fascinating new technology.

THE SOCIAL IMPACT OF WEARABLE TECHNOLOGY

While wearable technology and immersive technologies are currently moving along their own parallel paths, is there any chance that these technologies will meet in the middle at some point in the not-so-distant future? And if so, what are the social consequences of living in a

AN INTRODUCTION TO WEARABLE TECHNOLOGY

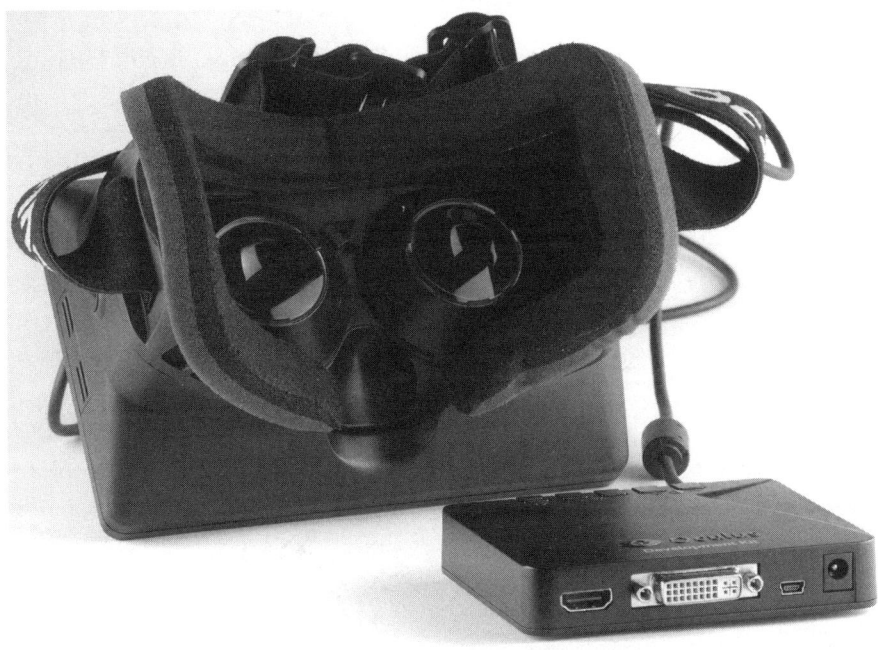

The Oculus Rift VR viewer. Photo by Sebastian Stabinger, Flickr.

"blended" world, where physical reality, augmented reality, and virtual reality overlap one another and could conceivably interact across the layers as well? I only jokingly refer to using Google Glass in public as "wearing the future on my face," but as these various forms of wearable technologies become more ubiquitous, we are going to find ourselves in a strange and unfamiliar world where the time-old notions of the personal and the private—especially where data is concerned—will become so blurred as to be virtually (pardon the pun) meaningless. Librarians will need to adapt to this changed personal digital landscape, not just in being able to deliver information to patrons via their preferred mobile or wearable platforms, but also to offer better guides and signposts to meet our patrons halfway in this strange, new blended world.

NOT ALL ABOUT THAT (GOOGLE) GLASS

Even from just a casual glance at the table of contents, it will become clear that many of the best practices and projects herein are focused on Google Glass. This is not so much an endorsement of Google over other wearable-technology devices as it is an acknowledgment that Glass is the only viable alternative for a full wearable computing device. At the time of this writing, however, Google has announced that effective January 2015 the Glass Explorers program would be coming to a close, ending the two-year experimental trial phase involving the prototype version of the Google Glass device ("Google Glass," Google+, January 15, 2015, https://plus.google.com/).

Most if not all of the devices being developed for release in the next one to two years will likely run on a similar platform (i.e., some brand of iOS in the case of Apple products or the Android platform for Google and other devices) and will likely be tethered to one's smartphone. So, although the projects in chapter 5 involving Google Glass have been designed using the Glass Explorer edition of the device, they should be easily adaptable to future consumer iterations of Glass or other future wearable computers that may become commercially available in the not-so-distant future.

2

GETTING STARTED WITH WEARABLE TECHNOLOGY

The Current State of Wearable Technology

WE HAVE ONLY JUST BEGUN

It is important to note that as of writing this book, the field of wearable technology currently available to the public is still rather narrow in scope. Aside from Google Glass—which over the past two years has moved from a closed, invite-only alpha-testing period to an open, public beta-testing phase of broader commercial availability, and then back again to a closed development cycle in anticipation of a future public release—and the category of personal fitness trackers (i.e., FitBits and similar devices), which has admittedly enjoyed a good deal of mainstream success, there are only a few other items available on the consumer electronics market that can be properly considered wearable technology. To be fair, this is about to change. For example, Samsung has recently had a demo of its own "Samsung Gear VR" viewer at various Best Buy retail stores (Jon Fingas, "Best Buy Will Let You Try Samsung's Gear VR in Stores on February 8," Engadget, February 7, 2015, http://www.engadget.com/); and at a January 2015 media event for the Windows 10 operating system, Microsoft introduced its "HoloLens" 3-D augmented-reality headset (Peter Bright, "Hands-On: Microsoft's HoloLens Is Flat-Out Magical," Ars Technica, January 22, 2015, http://arstechnica.com/).

At the same time Sony, Samsung, and other electronics manufacturers have launched their own smartwatches, and Google has even launched a software-development platform, called "Android Wear," which is specifically geared toward wearable-technology apps. But aside from the unexpected cult success of the Pebble smartwatch, which raised a record amount of money in its Kickstarter campaign, the public has been thus far lukewarm at best about adopting the smartwatch.

Why such a lack of enthusiasm? Again, the battery life on such devices is frequently mentioned, as is the lack of a robust application ecosystem, but perhaps the most damning criticism of wearable computing as a concept is that it can't replace the need to have one's smartphone on hand at all times. Not only does Google Glass and most smartwatches need a phone with which to pair in order to get a data connection, but also since wearable-tech devices only offer a small viewing space and limited options for user input, users frequently find themselves needing to consult their phones anyway, making such devices at least at the moment nothing more than an expensive filter or notification system for their default mobile device.

WEARABLE TECHNOLOGY'S EXISTENTIAL CRISIS

At heart this is the basic problem of wearable technology. Are these devices meant to replace one's smartphone or supplement it? Consumer electronics manufacturers of course want to sell future customers on the idea that wearable technology might one day completely obviate the need to carry around a smartphone in your pocket, but the reality is that even in the next three to five years it is extremely unlikely than any one device will carry the day in such fashion.

THE FUTURE IS WEARABLE

Nevertheless, the wearable-tech revolution is already taking place—in the laboratories of electronics manufacturers, the studios of fashion designers, and the hearts and minds (as well as other vital statistics) of consumers around the world. In the 2013 Higher Education edition of the "NMC Horizon Report," published jointly by the New Media Consortium and the EDUCAUSE Learning Initiative, wearable technology is identified as being an emerging technology of significant importance in the field of higher education over the next four to five years.

> One of the most compelling potential outcomes of wearable technology in higher education is productivity. Wearable technologies that could automatically send information via text, email, and social networks on behalf of the user, based on voice commands, gestures, or other indicators, would help students and educators communicate with each other, keep track of updates, and better organize notifications.

In their IDTechEx report "Wearable Technology 2014–2024: Technologies, Markets, Forecasts," authors Peter Harrop, Raghu Das, and Guillaume Chansin predict that the market for wearable tech will grow from over $14 billion in 2014 to over $70 billion in 2024, especially in the health-care sector, where wearable-technology devices will be able to make personal medicine, wellness, and fitness measureable and trackable on a personal level. The popularity of the Fitbit demonstrates that this aspect of the consumer potential of wearable technology is not to be overestimated. In a recent survey of over six thousand consumers in Australia, Canada, India, South Africa, the United Kingdom, and the United States, the technology consulting firm Accenture found that more than half of those polled expressed an interest in purchasing a wearable health or fitness tracker or application in the coming year. Interest in wearable technology for personal metrics and the "quantified self" was especially high among those polled under the age of thirty-five, as well as consumers living in India.

ONE RING TO RULE THEM ALL, OR INFINITE DIVERSITY IN INFINITE COMBINATIONS?

There remains, however, some ambiguity among consumers as to whether wearable technology should be its own beast—requiring its own separate purchase, care, and feeding—or whether wearable tech should live as an application within one's already expansive existing suite of personal electronics. Consider the Fitbit, by far the most popular personal activity tracker, comprising over 50 percent of all wearable fitness band sales, with 2.7 million bands shipped just in the first quarter of 2014 ("Fitbit Accounted for Nearly Half of Global Wearable Band Shipments in Q1 2014," Canalys, May 21, 2014, http://www.canalys.com/). At the same time, both sales of wearable smart bands (i.e., smartwatches, such as Pebble and Samsung Gear) have also skyrocketed, and downloads of fitness tracking and personal training applications for smartphones have reached such record high levels that traditional gyms are worried about the long-term impact on their business model (Tom DiChristopher, "Wearables: High Rents Pose a Challenge to Gym Operators," CNBC, January 10, 2015, http://www.cnbc.com/).

Have consumers settled upon whether they want one wearable-tech device or many? Almost a third of those six thousand consumers polled by Accenture say that they would prefer "having just one device housing all the functionality they need." Certainly the evolution of the wearable-tech market thus far has supported this element of personal choice in one's own wearable-tech platform, with core functionality and even popular applications replicated in parallel across wearable bands, smartwatches, and smartphones. Will this ambiguity persist when the next generation of wearable technology becomes cheap, flexible, and durable enough to embed within clothing itself, with smart clothing predicted to overtake sales of Fitbits and other personal fitness trackers by the end of 2016? (Samuel Gibbs, "Forget Smartwatches: Smartclothes Are the Future, Analysts Say," *Guardian*, November 18, 2014, http://www.theguardian.com/). Or will the technologies continue to develop and evolve in parallel to support a broader cross-section of adopters? Recent consumer history would suggest the latter answer is true, but perhaps wearable technology will soon reach a tipping point beyond which replicating its functionality on a smartphone is no longer something that the average users wants or needs.

A PRACTICAL DEFINITION OF WEARABLE TECHNOLOGY

The indeterminate and rapidly evolving current state of wearable technology also presents some basic taxonomic problems for the writing of this book (after all, we are librarians, so of course we would have to talk about taxonomy at some point)—that is, what should we include here as wearable technology, and what falls short of this definition for a book of this scope? I have used the following criteria for making this determination:

1. Openness of platform
2. Potential for library-based projects
3. Current availability to consumers

SINGLE-FUNCTION WEARABLE TECH

For example, the Fitbit is a form of wearable technology (produced by Fitbit Inc., located in San Francisco) that has actually been in widespread use for several years. Fitbit has specialized in creating small wearable devices that measure the daily physical activity of its wearer and then aggregate and track this data so that users can make more proactive informed decisions about their health and fitness. While this is by any objective standard a clear demonstration of the utility and mainstream appeal of wearable technology, the options for incorporating a Fitbit or other personal wearable tracker into your library's activities are limited due to the targeted scope of these device itself.

WEARABLE DIGITAL CAMERAS (GOPRO)—READY FOR YOUR CLOSE-UP

The GoPro camera (produced by GoPro Inc., located in San Mateo, California) is another example of wearable technology that has already been successfully adopted by the public—these personally mountable, rugged, and water-resistant cameras have been in use for more than a decade and have allowed millions of users to produce their own first-person videos of all manners of physical activities. Again, however, the single-purpose nature of the GoPro and other wearable cameras limits the range of activities for wearable-technology projects in your library. While this book will feature projects involving both wearable biometric devices such as the FitBit and wearable cameras such as the GoPro, ironically enough these items have already been sufficiently incorporated into your library patrons' lives already that there is less practical

The GoPro camera. Photo by Dave Dugdale, Flickr.

utility in trying to develop them as part of your wearable-technology program.

SMARTWATCHES—BACK TO THE FUTURE?

To those of us of a certain age, the smartwatch is the very embodiment of wearable technology, as it was the futuristic device of choice for such fictional heroes as Dick Tracy, who as early as the 1940s sported his iconic "Two-Way Wrist Radio" (upgraded to a two-way television in 1964) in his tireless campaign against the criminal masterminds of his city. This fascination with the potential of the smartwatch no doubt helped fuel the rise of the first commercially successful wearable computer and helped the various brands of calculator watches produced by Casio and other electronics manufacturers become ubiquitous during the 1980s. This same demographic has been waiting with bated breath for the fully computerized smartwatch to deliver on its promise ever since.

Smartwatches present a similar problem for this book in terms of applicability to library projects and scope. Although there are now more than a few viable smartwatch devices available for consumer purchase,

The Pebble smartwatch. *Source:* Pebble Press Pack 1. Pebble Technology.

as of yet these devices are still of limited use, although some applications have come to take more full advantage of a smartwatch's ability to send useful notifications based on timely location and other personal information processed from its wearer's environment. For example, the Pebble smartwatch (produced by the Pebble Technology Corporation in California) is a relatively affordable, wearable smartwatch device launched to the consumer market after a wildly successful Kickstarter campaign in 2012–2013 to crowd-fund its initial development. Units range from $99 for the basic model in plastic to $250 for a more rugged metal device, have a black and white display, and can sync with both iOS and Android mobile devices. The Pebble also has the advantage of boasting a phenomenal battery life, with devices able to operate for up to an entire week on a full charge. The Pebble has sold almost half a million devices since its commercial launch, and the Pebble app store now has over a thousand smartwatch applications. However, its lack of a touch-screen interface has made it susceptible to the next generation of competition in the smartwatch market niche, which includes the extremely powerful Galaxy Gear produced by Samsung and an Apple iOS-based smartwatch slated to hit the consumer electronics market in early 2015.

ENCOURAGING USE AND EXPERIMENTATION AMONG LIBRARY STAFF

Once you have established some basic familiarity with your new wearable-technology devices among your library staff, it is important to allow them ongoing access to these items as well, so they can also experiment and attempt to incorporate wearable technology into their own work. Google is famous for its "20% Time" policy, whereby the company expects employees to pursue their own projects for one day out of any given week. This philosophy should be extended as best as possible to any new devices you might add to your library. While it may be tempting to circulate Google Glass as much as possible to your patrons and loan it to other stakeholders who have demonstrated interest in developing the device as a research and instructional tool, I would argue that it is just as important to block out some time for your own staff members to play with Glass and other forms of wearable technology to see how they can best be utilized at public service desks and behind the scenes in your library's operations.

One of the ways to address this is to build enough redundancy into your wearable-technology loan program that you always have one device on hand for staff projects. Another is to encourage your staff to borrow your devices just like other library patrons. However you decide to proceed and support library staff development of wearable technology, as with fostering any kind of innovation in the library workplace you want to make sure that either your staff have the requisite skill in order to innovate or you provide resources for allowing library staff to quickly ascend the learning curve in order to maximize the development potential of any new technology or device.

CULTIVATING SUPPORT IN YOUR LIBRARY

As a library manager, I can't even count the amount of times that my staff or I have been introduced to a new application or device that clearly has potential for drastically improving or enhancing how we do our work but also requires significant investment of time and energy in order to realize that potential. Lucky is the library workplace where staff already have the skills on hand in order to take full advantage of such an opportunity, but what does a manager do when the staff enthusiasm is clear but the technological know-how is lacking?

First and foremost you want to cultivate a relationship with your library information technology (IT) support. Even if you are not able to provide the skills and resources necessary in order to get a wearable-technology project off the ground, it is possible that library IT might be able to assist you in some capacity. Also, if you work at a college or university, do not disregard two extremely important (and relatively inexpensive) resources you are likely to have on hand: your school's computer science department and student library assistants. Many academic libraries have successfully enlisted the help of their computer science or electrical engineering departments to assist them with large projects. For example, Brigham Young University partnered with their computer science department in order to help comprehensively assess and enhance the usability of their interlibrary-loan web presence, which required a significant amount of web programming and coding experience.

SEEK STRATEGIC PARTNERSHIPS IN YOUR COMMUNITY

You should consider similarly reaching out to your own faculty and students in this regard in order to leverage their expertise. Perhaps you could partner with a particular class in order to develop library-specific Glassware applications via the Android-based Glass Developers' Kit as a semester project? Many undergraduate groups also include some kind of technology support group for the student body. Consider enlisting these groups as well as potential developmental partners (this is in fact what we did here at Yale, approaching our Student Technology Collaborative as an equal partner in the Bass Glass Project as we had on other loanable technology initiatives).

Finally, do not discount the technological expertise you may already have on hand among your student library workers. At every academic library in which I've worked, our student employees are almost always more tech-savvy and knowledgeable about programming and scripting than regular full-time employees. The advantage of engaging your library student workforce is that because they are already familiar with library operations and therefore our unique needs for supporting library services, there is less of a learning curve in translating your developmental ideas into the requisite steps needed in order to craft a programming solution for your problem.

THE WEARABLE LIBRARIAN

We as librarians talk a lot about embedded librarianship, where librarians attempt to ensconce themselves outside of the library in order to maximize their own service reach and relevance to the academic setting. Consider the utility however of using this model to embed your own library-specific technology resources within your own workforce. Always be on the lookout for such latent potential among your ranks, as these library student employees already "get" libraries and are therefore your greatest assets in helping grow your own local innovation, such as making better use of wearable tech and other emerging technologies. You may not be able to wrangle enough time and resources out of your library IT department in order to support this kind of development, but can you hire a student expert in a project capacity over a semester or a summer in order to help get your project off the ground?

Even among our most technologically competent library staff, there is usually a gap preventing us from realizing projects such as incorporating wearable technology into our operations and services. Part of the gap is a function of time, whereas the other part of the gap is a function of knowledge. I've seen so many good ideas fall into this gap and never emerge to see the light of day again, not for a lack of enthusiasm or recognized potential impact but because there was no one in my organization who could take the idea and help us identify, plan, and execute the concrete steps needed to make that idea a reality. How do we foster this kind of innovation as library managers and administrators?

- We recognize first and foremost that the best new ideas come from practitioners and that we should always be engaging our library staff as potential engines of continuous improvement and development.
- We make time and space for our library staff to pursue new ideas, and we commit a portion of our resources to help develop these ideas if they show merit or developmental potential. Consider the

Harvard Library's very successful Library Lab project, which elicited library staff proposals for experimental applications and other technological innovation from across the entire university library system. This is a model worthy of emulation, even if on a smaller and more sustainable scale.
- We understand that leveraging existing external or internal resources can make the difference between a good idea that goes nowhere and a good idea put into practical use.
- We give our staff the license and encouragement to fail. Not every attempt at innovation will be successful, but the point of supporting this kind of constant experimentation is to create a culture among your library staff that shows that innovation and forward thinking are part of your core values. This to me is the most important thing you can do if you are in a position of library leadership, as while many people say that their workplace tolerates risk and does not penalize failure, talking the talk and walking the walk are often two separate things entirely. Experimentation means that you will not always see a "return" on your "investment"; failure means that you must have the courage to admit to your staff, your superiors, and your peers that something didn't work.

3

TOOLS AND APPLICATIONS

GLASSWARE AND OTHER WEARABLE-TECHNOLOGY APPLICATIONS

Glassware—Still under Development

Similar to other handheld and mobile devices, wearable technology depends heavily on applications for the majority of its functionality. Consider, for example, the Google Glass user interface:—although there is some limited onboard voice-command capability, a manual

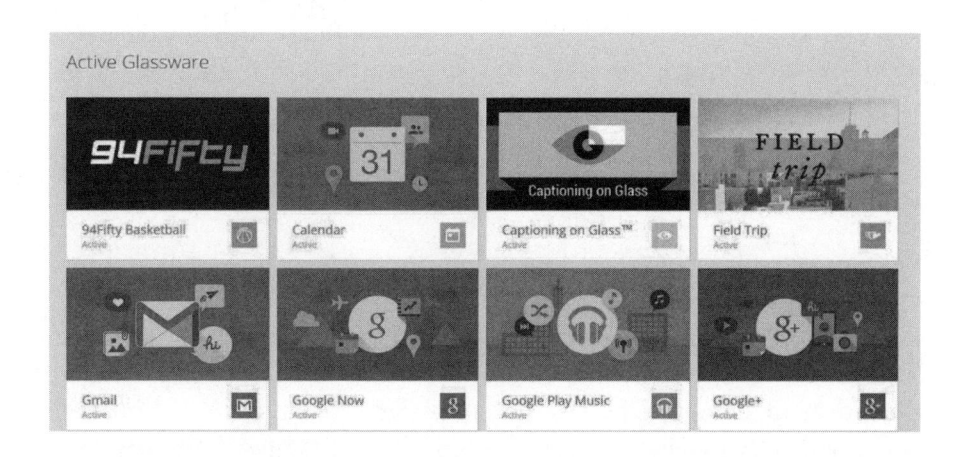

Glassware apps for Google Glass.

camera button, and an option to take a picture with a wink, the wearer navigates the device's operating system primarily by swiping up and down or front to back on the Glass frame. Applications for Google Glass—also known as Glassware—therefore must be designed specifically to the device in order to help facilitate access to existing web services and other mobile apps and to take advantage of Glass and other wearable technologies' specific strengths.

To this end, Google has developed and released a small but steadily growing body of Glassware applications that users can easily add to their device. As Google has encouraged independent programmers to develop applications for Glass by releasing the Glass Development Kit, there is also a rich ecosystem of third-party Glassware apps available as well, although these unofficial applications are at the moment slightly more difficult to load onto your device and are more likely to be unstable as they are not supported directly by Google. Here we will briefly survey the current landscape of Glassware apps, starting with the most important application for Google Glass: the MyGlass app.

MyGlass Overview

In order to set up your Google Glass device for the first time, you'll need to install and run the MyGlass application on your smartphone or other mobile device. The MyGlass app serves as your primary interface for your Glass device, allowing you to manage your Bluetooth or data connection between devices, install or uninstall your existing Glassware applications, and even send a factory reset command to your device if for whatever reason your Glass becomes unresponsive and cannot be reset manually.

Screencasting Google Glass

Perhaps the most important function in the MyGlass application, however, is the screencast capability, which allows you to turn your smartphone or tablet into a mirror for your Glass device. The screencast function displays on your mobile device screen whatever is displaying in the prism of Google Glass (a function that can be extremely useful when presenting Glass to a large group, either in a live demonstration or a "petting zoo" event; more about how to make the most use out of this capability later in the book, in chapter 5). And the touchscreen of your mobile device will also respond to the basic touch commands you use on the Google Glass frame in order to navigate the device's operating system, so if you are feeling uncomfortable using the frame-based gestures or for whatever reason you feel the device is not responding naturally to your input, you can use the mirroring function when screencasting in order access the device's operating system.

Third-Party Applications and "Sideloading"

Enabling or disabling officially supported Glassware is simple—using the MyGlass application, simply toggle the app on or off, and your device will install or uninstall the application the next time it is actively paired with your smartphone or connected to the Internet via wi-fi. Third-party Glassware applications, however, must be installed manually, also known as "sideloading"—this includes any of your own applications you would like to design for your Google Glass device. If you are familiar with installing software manually on an Android device, because Glass runs on a specialized form of the Android operating system the sideloading process is almost identical for loading third-party Glassware; but if you've never attempted this before, sideloading can seem like an extremely daunting task even to an otherwise tech-savvy individual (such as yours truly). There are several guides online that will walk you through how to sideload an application onto your Glass device, but the basic step-by-step operation is as follows:

1. Enable debugging mode on your Google Glass.
2. Plug your device into a computer via USB.
3. Download the Google Glass Android drivers.
4. Modify the drivers to recognize Glass as a USB Android device.
5. Download and run ADB (Android Debug Bridge)—this will serve as your command-line interface for sideloading and installing third-party Glassware onto your device.

Note: Please be advised that sideloading any Android device—including Google Glass—with an untested third-party application always involves some measure of risk. Glassware that has not been sufficiently tested or debugged, if sideloaded onto your device, can cause it to behave erratically or even "brick" (i.e., cause it to stop working entirely) your Glass.

Be sure to read the Glassware application reviews extensively when considering whether or not to sideload a new app to your Google Glass. Many third-party Glassware applications are not updated as frequently as the officially supported/endorsed apps, with the result that when Google pushes out an upgrade to the Glass operation system, the Glassware can fail unless modified and rereleased by the original developer. Also, if you or your patrons are programming your own Glassware, be sure to test your application virtually before attempting to run it live on the device.

TOOLS AND APPLICATIONS FOR SMARTWATCHES

Pebble Smartwatch Apps—Three Thousand Applications and Growing

The Pebble smartwatch, which was the brainchild of a successful Kickstarter campaign, was an attempt to realize the science-fiction potential of the digital wristwatch, which had been dangling like a carrot in front of wearable-technology enthusiasts since the Dick Tracy comics of old. With a simple design, an intuitive interface, and (perhaps most importantly) an open developers' kit to inspire third-party application support, no sooner had the Pebble launched than it had a robust selection of apps for users to install on their new smartwatches. In just a little over two years, the total amount of Pebble smartwatch applications now exceeds three thousand, with a host of different fitness tracking applications, GPS navigation aids, notification applications that push important updates from your smartphone, games, RSS readers, and even scaled-down versions of popular Android or iOS applications such as Evernote.

Like most other existing forms of wearable technology, the Pebble smartwatch pairs with your smartphone (both Android phones and iPhones are supported) using Bluetooth in order to run its applications. Once paired, the user then downloads the official Pebble application either via iTunes or Google Play in order to manage and download your apps. Please note that there are also some additional standalone Pebble applications for both Android and iOS; although these applications can be installed and run as independent applications on your smartphone, they will require your Pebble smartphone to be turned on and running in order to function.

Don't Like Your Options? Then Code Your Own App!

One of the most intriguing and inspiring aspects of the Pebble smartwatch is that not only have the owners/creators opened the developers' kit to third-party programmers but also it actually encourages nondevelopers to explore the Pebble SDK as well, posting step-by-step guides about how to code your own Pebble smartwatch applications! The Pebble developer website has a beginners' tutorial on designing your own custom Pebble watchface, which not only walks you through the process of coding a simple app from start to finish but also explains the entire process in layperson's terms so that someone with limited programming skills or no coding experience whatsoever can follow along and understand how the basic interface operates ("Build Your Own Watchface," Pebble, accessed April 10, 2015, http://developer.getpebble.com/).

Once users have successfully coded their own custom watchface, the tutorial continues to build on more complex programming, including how to add dynamic web/online content to your application from your smartphone. Truly this is a labor of love on the part of Pebble's developers, who could have very well left the programming to hard-core enthusiasts and other third-party commercial coders. By not only opening up the Pebble SDK but also explaining how it works on the most basic level, the Pebble smartwatch successfully lures the do it yourself (DIY) tech crowd back into the fold by co-opting them into the process of coding their own sci-fi wish fulfillment.

Other Smartwatch Tools and Applications (Samsung, Moto, and LG): Too Many Platforms and Not Enough Apps

There has been a proliferation of smartwatches coming onto the market over the past year or so, offering what must seem like a bewildering array of choices and options to the would-be neophyte wearable-technology consumer. In the past year alone, Samsung has released not one or two but six different smartwatches, on two separate operating plat-

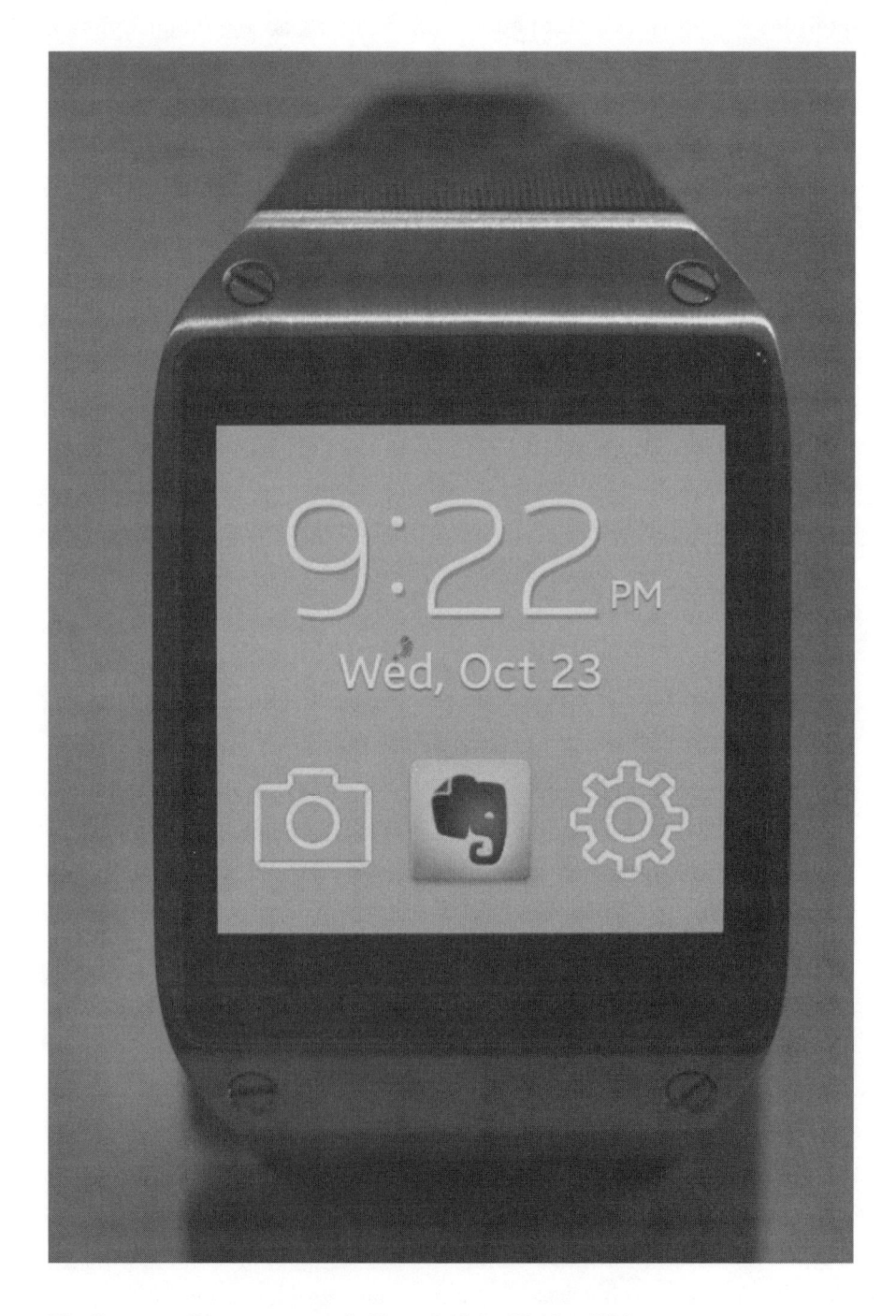

The Samsung Gear smartwatch. Photo by John Biehler, Flickr.

forms no less—the Google-based Android Wear OS and the open-source Tizen platform. With the exception of the Pebble smartwatch, which runs its own operating system, and the soon-to-be-released Apple Watch, which will have a platform based off of iOS, virtually all smartwatches currently on the market are running either some version of Android Wear or Tizen.

Why are there already two competing platforms in a form of wearable technology that is so brand new we're not even entirely sure what we want out of it yet? The seeds of this bifurcation are apparently a rift between Samsung and Google. Whereas the search giant wanted Samsung to wait for the Android Wear operating system to be sufficiently developed to support a wider consumer release for wearable tech, the electronics giant Samsung, wary about missing an opportunity to make early inroads into this developing market, chose not to wait for Google and released several devices on the open-source Tizen operating system as its default platform instead (Jon Fingas, "Google Reportedly Confronted Samsung over Its Approach to Smartwatches," Engadget, July 19, 2014, http://www.engadget.com/).

THE CUTTING-EDGE LIBRARIAN'S DILEMMA

This fragmented developmental landscape is in part a problem endemic to all forms of mobile technology but is especially acute for anyone who is trying to programmatically support these new devices. For example, how do librarians choose a platform on which to deliver their content and enhance their services? Patrons have already begun to demand that their library meet them at least halfway on their own technology, whether it's allowing them to access resources online from the comfort of their own desktops or laptops or letting them check out e-books on their own Amazon Kindle. We have enjoyed the luxury of developing our virtual and mobile library presences in something of a vacuum. Even now many librarians are still happily patting themselves on the back for designing web content that can render just as well on a smartphone, as if this is something that we shouldn't have been doing in the first place since the mobile revolution began years ago.

The mainstreaming of wearable technology will make our smartphone usability headaches look trivial in comparison, however, as our patrons will soon expect to be able to interact with the library using these devices on a much more granular level. If a patron can check an e-book out to their Kindle, why couldn't they check out a physical book from the stacks using their smartwatch and a barcode scanner or near field communication (NFC) tag? Why shouldn't they be able to receive alerts on their wearable-tech devices calling their attention to relevant virtual or online content (such as location-specific finding aids) as they move through the actual library space? The fact that we must support several different wearable-technology platforms at once is a challenge, to be sure, but one that libraries and librarians ignore at their own peril.

SAMSUNG GEAR (TIZEN)

Getting Started with Samsung Gear Smartwatches

The Samsung Gear family of smartwatches, which run using the open-source Tizen operating system, allows you to manage your smartwatch applications through the Samsung Gear application on your smartphone.

1. Select Samsung Gear Apps.
2. Select Category tab, and choose your category.
3. When you have found an app you'd like to add to your phone, touch the FREE button to download the application (you will need a Samsung account in order to proceed).
4. Read any app permissions if required, and then touch Accept Conditions and download.
5. Your app, once downloaded and installed, will appear under the Gear Manager menu.

ANDROID WEAR

Getting Started with Android Wear Smartwatches

Android Wear is Google's own operating system for wearable technology. As with other wearable-tech platforms, Android Wear is managed

TOOLS AND APPLICATIONS

through an application that you download onto your phone and not the smartwatch itself. While some Android Wear smartwatch applications can be installed directly onto the watch itself, the key difference is that instead of installing and managing applications on the phone itself, Android Wear serves as the intermediary between the applications you have already installed and are running on your Android smartphone and your smartwatch. This concept can take a little getting used to at first, especially in the way that Android Wear pushes information, status updates, and other notifications to your smartwatch.

It's All in the Cards

Have you ever noticed that when you perform a search on Google, there is an index-card-sized summary of your search results on the upper-right-hand side of the page? This is the basic unit of information for the Android Wear platform: the card. If you have Google Now enabled on your smartphone, you will have already noticed that Google is using cards to attempt to extract the information it thinks you really want from your search history and present it in a useful summary format that has been optimized for mobile reviewing.

These notification cards are what is being managed by your Android Wear application and pushed from your smartphone to your smartwatch. Therefore how many notification cards are being pushed from your phone to your watch ultimately depends on the notification set-

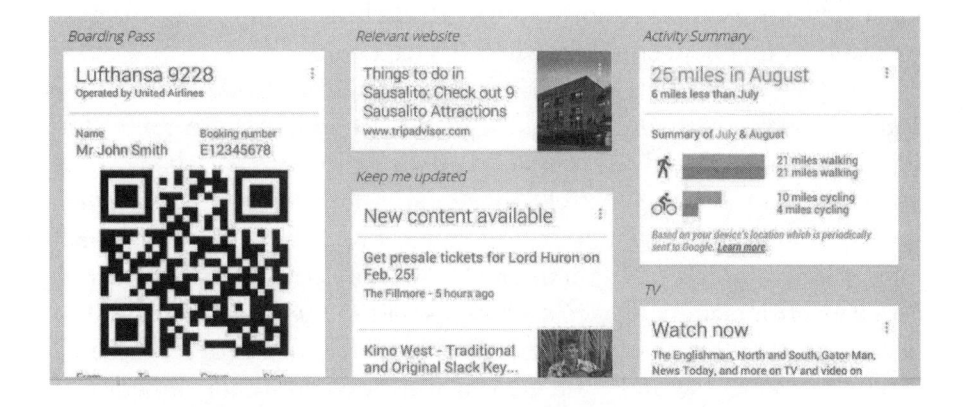

An example of Google Now and cards as the basic level of search results.

tings you have configured for your smartphone. You may find that notifications you were happy to receive on your phone arrive too frequently for your watch, or that there are certain applications on your phone whose notifications you don't necessarily wish to see on your smartwatch. The Android Wear application on your phone allows you to selectively mute app notifications using the following instructions:

1. Launch the Android Wear application on your smartphone.
2. Go to Settings.
3. Select "Mute app notifications."
4. Manage your list of smartphone applications you'd like to mute.

OTHER SMARTWATCH TOOLS

To NFC or Not NFC? That Is the Question

Although the smartwatch is limited by its small screen and lack of a keyboard or other easy-to-use user interface for input, its ability to sync with another mobile device and read NFC tags makes it a perfect candidate for any project involving NFC tags in your library. Imagine being able to provide on-the-spot information at various locations in your stacks, for example, or delivering event notifications to your patrons by tapping a location adjacent to the library venue. Here we will look at a simple project involving setting up geolocation for your library stacks, based on call number ranges. These navigational checkpoints, once set up, could be used with not only smartwatches but also any form of wearable or mobile technology with GPS capability.

If you've ever seen a kid play the videogame Skylanders or Disney Infinity (or played it yourself—these games are fun!), where collectible figurines can be placed on a physical surface in order to add them to the gameplay, then you've seen NFC in action. A form of short-range wireless communication, near field communication relies on a very small loop antenna, which can then interact with a similar antenna or with an active electromagnetic device such as a smartphone when brought into close proximity or physical contact. This allows the active device to "read" the NFC tag and even exchange data in the other direction—that is, from the active device to the tag. NFC tags are currently in use

TOOLS AND APPLICATIONS   31

An example of a QR code paired with an NFC tag. Photo by Clive Darra, Flickr.

in many commercial settings, from smart cards used for hotel room keys to "one-touch payment" or "tap-to-pay" kiosks, as well as the aforementioned video game applications. Although there are many potential projects for implementing near field communication features to your library, let us start with something relatively simple—taking the preceding project to set up QR codes in the library and transforming them into

NFC tagged locations as well so they can be read by either NFC-enabled smartphones or wearable technology such as smartwatches.

Outcome Unclear—Ask Again Later

Near field communication is something of an enigma for mobile devices. While there are many potential applications for NFC, especially in the field of wearable technology (one of our library projects later in this book will feature a project involving NFC tags), consumer electronics manufacturers have been slow to incorporate this functionality into smartphones and other devices. Even those wearable-tech devices that do have NFC capabilities built in may be restricted in their use by the hardware's design—for example, although the iPhone 6 comes with NFC, it can only be used in conjunction with the new "Apple Pay" functionality that allows customers to pay for goods and services at participating retailers simply by tapping their phone at the payment kiosk.

It would be difficult to categorize which mobile and wearable-technology devices currently support NFC and in what capacity, especially as what may be true at the time of writing this book may no longer be the case by the time you are reading it. Instead, I would recommend researching the specific NFC capabilities of any given wearable tech and making your purchasing decisions accordingly. The amount of patron education that may or may not be required in order to instruct them in how to use the NFC features in their own wearable-technology devices or those you loan to them remains to be seen.

NFC Tags versus GPS

Indoor geolocation is a difficult problem to solve. Since traditional handheld GPS relies on a combination of satellite-based positioning and a reliable cell phone signal, bringing turn-by-turn navigation inside a building can easily be complicated by cellular reception issues. While some organizations and companies have attempted to solve this problem by adding cellular connectivity indoors, not only is this a costly endeavor but also it only works for one network provider at a time. As a result, many developers have turned to using indoor wi-fi networks in order to provide geolocation services, often known as "indoor position-

TOOLS AND APPLICATIONS 33

ing services or indoor GPS." Apple's iBeacon is a popular indoor positioning platform, and Google is working on their own indoor mapping project called Google Tango that could "see" the inside of the building just as a Microsoft Xbox Kinect can read the motion of people in a room. But both of these approaches have their own strengths and weaknesses as well, especially when one attempts to apply them to library spaces. Aside from letting Google drive a Street View mapping car through your stacks, what's the best way to add geolocation to your library, given the additional considerations of cost, technical expertise required, and the return on such an investment of said time, energy, and know-how?

Clearly QR codes and NFC tags are both extremely economical ways to augment one's physical library with virtual online functionality, as they require very little overhead to implement and almost nothing to maintain on an ongoing basis, aside from the occasional update or replacement of signs as the intersection of physical and virtual content changes or moves. However, in order to maximize their effectiveness, both QR codes and NFC tags require some education on the part of the library patron. For example, QR codes can still only be scanned by most devices (including Google Glass) by downloading and installing an application specifically designed to scan and read QR codes; on the other hand, while NFC tags can be read by almost any smartphone's onboard hardware, library patrons need to enable this ability in their device's settings, as this option is usually turned off by default. Explaining how to enable these two functions in order to take full advantage of one's virtual library presence is an important factor in the success or failure of any project involving QR codes or NFC tags, so consider adding some brief instructions at a central point of patron access, such as your reference or information desk, or your library's home page or newsletter.

4

LIBRARY EXAMPLES AND CASE STUDIES

WEARABLE TECHNOLOGY IN ACADEMIC LIBRARIES

Claremont University Library

Letting the Patron Drive Wearable Technology

I had the good fortune of being able to speak to Char Booth, director of Research, Teaching, and Learning Services at the Claremont Colleges Library. Through Char's efforts—and those of her colleague Dani Brecher—Claremont was able to launch a Google Glass loan program through the library system in the fall of 2013. Char describes the interest in Glass at Claremont to be "pretty intense," so much so that they were able to justify the purchase of a second device shortly after starting the loan program. Instructional technology isn't particularly emphasized at the Claremont Colleges, so Char suspects that the Claremont community saw Google Glass as a real opportunity to play with cutting-edge technology and incorporated it into their teaching, learning, and research so "people have really gone with it." This would also explain the surprisingly wide group of departments curious about using the device.

Circulating Google Glass at Claremont

Claremont employs a "nonselective" proposal process for scheduling and loaning their Glass devices. Prospective patrons fill out a form, and the Claremont library staff uses this information to find an ideal time during the semester to circulate Google Glass to the patron. Patrons are able to borrow the device for a week at a time, with some renewals possible depending on demand. This fairly nonrestrictive circulation policy has seemed to encourage experimentation among Claremont's patrons and promote assessment by library staff administering the Glass loan program. A week also seems to be an adequate amount of time for new users to master the learning curve for Google Glass. While Claremont does not require the faculty, students, and the staff to share some kind of final end product or deliverable resulting from their having borrowed Google Glass, they do ask them to participate in panel discussions about the program, and students have shared a lot of their own experiences through social media and other independent outlets.

Troubleshooting and Support

Since Claremont's IT department is contracted, development and support for Google Glass at the library is informal and library led. Although on the one hand this has been empowering for Claremont's Glass users, as both the librarians and patrons have been encouraged to provide their own basic support and troubleshooting, lack of dedicated local support has meant that there has not yet been much opportunity for developing Glass beyond its basic on-board functionality—that is, coding apps or customizing the devices beyond the default settings. Claremont does hope to include Google Glass in a future "hack-a-thon," during which they would ask tech-savvy members of the student body to spend a weekend intensively coding specifically for the device.

For the library's part, however, Char feels that rather than spend time, money, and resources on trying to anticipate and create applications for wearable technology such as Glass, the best possible thing libraries can do is to encourage its patrons to interact with new technologies and explore what they mean. An important part of administering Claremont's Google Glass loan program has been "not being stubborn about attempting to develop it" or pretending that wearable technology is all about libraries. In fact, if the library were the sole user for devices such as Glass, Char says, "then this would have been a very limited project indeed."

LIBRARY EXAMPLES AND CASE STUDIES

Wearable Tech and the Research Library Mission

Instead, by offering such items as wearable technology, the library has an opportunity to create a space where its users have a safe space for experimentation and play, which is wholly consistent with the library's mission of supporting the research and education experience. Loanable technology programs also advance the cause of intellectual freedom, as by purchasing these devices and making them available to the broadest possible group of borrowers, libraries are able to absorb the cost and therefore some of the financial risk associated with attempting to familiarize oneself with and master new forms of technology. Especially in the case of such a rapidly developing market as wearable tech, it can be confusing as to which devices are worth one's investment of time and money. By absorbing the initial start-up cost, the library can remove this guesswork.

Google Glass at the Yale University Library (Bass Glass)

Our own Google Glass loan program here at Yale University began in January 2014, when the library partnered with the Instructional Technology Group (ITG) and the Student Technology Collaborative (STC) in order to purchase a device to loan on a trial basis. As I had already mentioned in the preface of this book, I was selected as one of Google's inaugural class of Glass Explorers and thought the best possible use of such an invitation would be to share it with my colleagues at the library. Since the Bass undergraduate library already had an existing successful loanable Media Equipment collection, Google Glass seemed to be a perfect addition to this program, so we contacted the ITG and STC, who were the other partners in the Bass Media Equipment program, to see if they would be interested in experimenting with circulating this new wearable-technology device as well.

One Device, Three Partners—Google Glass, or the Treasure of the Sierra Madre?

Our first challenge was ensuring that all three of the partners would get sufficient time with their investment so that we could ascertain Google Glass's strengths and weaknesses and anticipate any potential problems in loaning the device out to our faculty, students, and staff. At the time, the Bass Media Equipment collection was an extremely successful and well-administered library technology loan program, so we felt that if we were going to add Google Glass to the list of items that circulated out of this collection, we needed to make sure that we could ensure a similar high level of service and reliability that library patrons had come to expect when borrowing other Bass Media Equipment items. As a result we almost immediately decided that the best way to loan the device at least during this first phase of the pilot was to circulate it on a project proposal basis, rather than allowing faculty, students, and staff to reserve it and borrow it on a first come, first served basis as we did with other Bass Media Equipment items.

The reason for this was simple: at the launch of the program, we only had one device. Also, since the Glass Explorers program was still in a closed invite-only beta period at the time, it was unclear whether we'd be able to secure a replacement in the case that a patron failed to return the device or accidentally lost it. As a result, the "Bass Glass" partners (as we were calling ourselves) were very reluctant to let the device go out in an unmediated fashion during this inaugural period, and instead we shared it internally among our various stakeholders—bringing it to demonstrations and staging "petting zoo" events, and setting up a trial loan to a faculty member in the arts department with whom the group had successfully partnered in the past in incorporating iPads into the classroom.

More Devices, Less Risk

After announcing the addition of Google Glass to the Bass Media Equipment program, we were approached by two members of the Yale community who had also been chosen as candidates for the Glass Explorer program but who had decided not to purchase the devices—both of these individuals kindly offered to give us their invitations so that we could add them to our own collection instead. For the Bass Glass group, this was perfect timing, as we were about to begin accepting proposals from Yale faculty, students, and staff for long- and short-term loan proposals for borrowing Google Glass. Having three devices in our collection would help us juggle our schedule and expand availability to the largest possible audience of interested patrons—it also helped alleviate the risk of only having one device to loan and gave us some added flexibility if for whatever reason one of the devices needed troubleshooting or even replacement (which has already happened twice since launching the program). This put us on the best possible footing for beginning our loan program in earnest.

Summer Vacation through Glass

Our inaugural loan period was during the summer of 2014, when we loaned our Glass devices out to several Yale community members on a series of long-term and short-term projects. Prospective projects proposals were submitted through a webform available on the Bass Media Equipment webpage and were evaluated by the group on the basis of practicality, technological feasibility, and merit. Applicants were asked to explain how Google Glass was an integral part of their proposed use of the device; while we were fine with project proposals that sought to explore the capabilities of Glass in various capacities, the more concrete and actionable the proposal, the more likely we were to select it for the loan program. Applicants who simply wanted to play around with Google Glass were deferred until we decided to add a freely circulating device to the Bass Media collection. Also, applicants who wanted to borrow Glass primarily for its audiovisual recording capabilities were encouraged to borrow one of our GoPro wearable cameras, which were available for regular unrestricted loan. The summer project proposal process resulted in several long- and short-period loans and was deemed successful enough to merit repeating the same selection process for the fall and spring semesters of the upcoming academic year.

Lessons Learned: HIPAA, African Dinosaur Safaris, and Fragile Development

HIPAA Nevertheless, getting our Glass loan program in to a smoothly running groove involved more than a few halts and starts. Our first major obstacle was determining whether or not Google Glass could be used by projects that were proposed by members of the Yale Medical community due to HIPAA (Health Insurance Portability and Accountability Act), which requires strict patient privacy protocols when working with medical records or other sensitive patient information. We discuss HIPAA in chapter 6, but it bears repeating that while straight out of the box Google Glass is not a HIPAA-compliant device, there are companies in the health-care technology field that have already partnered with Google in order to modify the stock Glass model so it can be made to comply with HIPAA requirements—(please refer to chapter 6, "Tips and Tricks," for more information). However, since we did not have one of these custom HIPAA-compliant Glass devices, we were obliged to reject any project proposal from our Medical School faculty, students, and staff if they were proposing to work directly with actual patients.

Have Glass, Will Travel? Our second major hurdle was deciding whether or not we'd be willing to let one of our Glass devices out of the country, or ship one overseas if the project proposal seemed compelling enough. One of our summer project proposals came from a graduate student in paleontology who wanted to bring Glass on-site to a dig in Africa over the summer to use the device as part of a geolocation and image-recognition project for dinosaur fossils. Now really, how much more exciting can you get than Google Glass plus dinosaurs? Despite the fact that our selection committee was extremely impressed with the proposal and interested in choosing this graduate student as one of our inaugural summer Bass Glass users, we have several concerns about this particular project. How would Google Glass fare going through airport security? We had seen some accounts of people traveling internationally with the device and running into a bit of confusion here and there with the Transportation Security Administration (TSA), and the last thing we wanted to have happen was for one of our devices to be confiscated en route to Africa. Were there any special liability insurance considerations for the patron that we'd have to clarify before loaning the device overseas?

As a rule we require anyone wishing to travel internationally with a circulating item from the Bass Media Equipment collection to sign a travel contract and submit proof of insurance before leaving the country. We decided this would be adequate for library patrons borrowing Google Glass as well, but at the time the Glass Explorers program was still in a closed beta and, even if insurance did cover the patron's and our loss, it was not clear whether we'd be able to replace the device if lost, damaged, or destroyed. Also, would there be adequate cellular or wi-fi connectivity at the dig site in order to take advantage of Glass's unique features? Despite the attraction of loaning Google Glass to such an interesting, high-profile project, we wanted to make sure that the patron would actually be able to use the device on-site, or recommend a different digital imaging solution if not. We were concerned with being able to support and assist with troubleshooting Glass from several thousand miles and more than half a dozen time zones away as well. In the end we decided that sending the device to Africa was worth all of the risks and concerns; unfortunately, the timing of the excavation project proved to be the ultimate limiting factor, with the result that we weren't able to provide the device in time for the applicant to make use of it at the dig site. However, we hope that the graduate student applies next year, because again, who doesn't like the idea of digging up dinosaurs through Google Glass?

Always Get a Spare Glass Our final major learning experience from our summer pilot loan program for Bass Glass was learning that, for all of the device's purported ruggedness, it was in fact easy for Google Glass to end up out of commission. I suppose one of the inherent risks of beta testing an experimental wearable-technology device is that given enough time, you will doubtless end up finding exciting new ways to break it that neither the manufacturer nor your peer group will have ever experienced themselves—for our part, we managed to rack up enough man-hours using Glass over the summer of 2014 to find two such hitherto-undiscovered methods of breakage, much to our own and the Google Glass Support Team's exasperation (and, at times, bemusement). In retrospect, having multiple devices on hand turned out to be of critical importance, as we were able to keep loaning Glass for our patrons' projects even while one device was in the shop for repairs or replacement. To be sure, we were fortunate to be working at an institution that could afford such an investment, but any library that is thinking about adding an expensive item like Google Glass to its loanable wearable-tech collection should consider purchasing at least one additional device in order to anticipate the inevitable trials and tribulations associated with owning experimental technology.

"Okay, Glass, Tell Me What We Should Do with You."

As one of the people primarily responsible for bringing Google Glass to the Yale University Library, I was probably the most intent on demonstrating to my supervisor and our library administration that their investment in wearable technology would be of tangible benefit to our library and its stakeholders—if not immediately then shortly after we acquired our Glass devices. I think trying to show a return on investment is a fairly common concern for anyone who tries to bring new technologies into the library, wearable or otherwise, but especially so in the case of a technology that hasn't quite found its home in the hearts and minds of mainstream consumers and (in the case of Google Glass) one that has been an object of so much scorn and ridicule from various quarters. I had quickly imagined scenarios in which the library could attempt to incorporate Glass into its operations—from using it to enable roving reference workers to using the image-recognition technology to assist in shelf-reading and to employing the devices in our "Scan and Deliver" electronic document delivery service so that staff members could scan books and journals right on the spot in the stacks.

While none of these ideas were bad, and may very well find their implementation in the library at some point in the future, after the benefit of several months of hindsight I realized that my fears were misplaced and that just as Claremont University had learned, the most powerful thing a library can do with new technologies is to create a safe space within which your patrons can experiment with these items, and in doing so help you understand how something like wearable technology can be of practical utility to your library's research and education mission. To me this was something of an epiphany, as in my duties I've always been the person actively seeking out ways to add new services or improve our existing library systems by staying on top of trends in technology and adopting improvements or best practices from our peers. The thought of adding something like Google Glass to our collections without a clear sense of how it should be used almost induced a sense of panic in me at first, but now I understand that the best way to find wearable tech's "purpose" in the library is to share it with as wide an audience as possible,stand back, and see what our community makes of it.

WEARABLE TECHNOLOGY IN PUBLIC LIBRARIES

Skokie Public Library

From Playable Tech to Wearable Tech

In 2009 the Skokie Public Library in Illinois established its Digital Media Lab, where library community members can access a sophisticated suite of hardware and software to assist them in the recording, editing, and production of digital music and video projects. The "DML" has proved to be an overwhelmingly popular and successful example of the library as creative space, so much so that other libraries have sought to emulate Skokie's model. As Mikael Jacobsen and Carolyn Anthony observe in their article "Build Your Own Digital Media Lab" (*Digital Shift*, November 8, 2011, http://www.thedigitalshift.com/), "As costs decrease and ease of use increases, it seems natural that the library would make this equipment and software available. It is still prohibitive for many, if not most, people to purchase high-end Macs, microphones, musical keyboards, green screens, professional-grade software, and other tools."

While much of the equipment at the Digital Media Lab is meant for on-site use, certain devices may be checked out of the library and borrowed for several days at a time. This includes three GoPro HD HERO2: Outdoor Edition wearable cameras. The GoPro has insinuated itself into many loanable equipment inventories at libraries (both public and academic) and as such is one of the easiest and most affordable ways to support wearable technology in your library.

Arapahoe Library District

Through the (Google) Glass, Past the (Oculus) Rift, and into the Future

When considering the role of public libraries in the twenty-first century, Michelle Cingrani, communications specialist at the Arapahoe Library District in Colorado, does not mince words. "The libraries of today are not buildings filled with dusty books and carefully indexed microfiche," she writes, "but libraries are offering the latest books, e-resources, online music and streaming media, as well as advanced and sometimes inaccessible technology—like Google Glass—for library patrons. ALD has made it a priority to ensure that difficult-to-access technology is readily available for our patrons—like Google Glass, 3-D printing, Leap Motion, an Oculus Rift Virtual Reality Headset, and video and music production studios at libraries" ("The Arapahoe Library District Is Talking Tech," Urban Libraries Council, accessed April 20, 2015, http://www.urbanlibraries.org/).

The concept of rebranding libraries—and public libraries in particular—as "innovation centers" is no longer a revolutionary idea for our discipline, but how exactly to put this ambitious idea into practice can still be a challenge for many libraries. The Arapahoe Library District approaches this problem much in the same spirit as we did here at Yale and just as our counterparts did at the Claremont Library, that is, by acquiring new technologies and creating a space where library patrons can discover and interact with them without necessarily having to purchase such experimental (and potentially expensive) devices with their own funds. Embracing a "try before you buy" philosophy behind showcasing cutting-edge electronics and wearable technology may seem unusual for a traditionally noncommercial institution such as a public library. After all, we are talking about libraries here, and not Apple stores.

The Library and Technological Literacy

Consider however the benefits to offering an environment where the public can explore the latest technology without having to worry about direct or indirect sales pressure from their guides, but instead where they receive the same kind of informed guidance that they have come to expect from their librarians in other respects, such as reference, reader's advisory, and other areas of public service expertise around which libraries are built. "Unlike a retail store, ALD is not in the business of selling technology, so library staff can offer advice and support on a variety of devices and technologies," Michelle Cingrani writes. "Technological literacy is another form of literacy, and libraries have always been in the business of developing an informed and literate community" ("Google Glass: Try before You Buy Technology," Public Libraries Online, January 8, 2014, http://publiclibrariesonline.org/)

To this end, the Arapahoe Library District has invested a significant amount of time, money, and expertise into supporting a wide range of emerging technologies within its library spaces. Here I will look more closely at two of their investments: their purchase of Google Glass and the Oculus Rift virtual-reality headset. Arapahoe acquired a Google Glass device as part of the Glass Explorers program, having sent a successful video entry to the Glass development team via Twitter using the "#ifihadglass" hashtag (see the winning video on YouTube: Nick Taylor, "#ifihadglass Arapahoe Library District," February 27, 2013, https://www.youtube.com/). The library district has shared its Google Glass with the community via a series of "Goggle at Google Glass" events (http://arapahoelibraries.org/googleglass), where anyone age six or older can try out the device. This kind of technology petting zoo event can be very successful, as it allows the widest range possible for library patrons to have a hands-on experience with new devices, rather than wait for one's turn in the library hold queue for a brand-new circulating item.

Oculus Rift and the Immersive Library

Another even more experimental form of wearable technology that Arapahoe has decided to support and explore is the Oculus Rift, a headset that provides an immersive 3-D virtual-reality experience when worn by the user. Each of the Arapahoe Library District's eight branches have one of the devices, where library patrons can reserve time to use the viewer and experience one of several simulation programs currently available. "We're trying to find things that could be of interest—we're not just trying to select random technology," Oli Sanidas, director of Digital Services for the Arapahoe Library District said. "We thought it would be interesting to show our patrons what does virtual reality look like in this day and age" (Clayton Woullard, "Curious About Oculus Rift Gaming Headset? Check It Out at Arapahoe Libraries," *Denver Post* YourHub, March 26, 2014, http://www.denverpost.com/).

On the Arapahoe Library District's Frequently Asked Questions page for Oculus Rift (http://arapahoelibraries.org/), they say the following:

> Q: Why does the library invest in technologies such as these?
> A: As a resource for the community, the library offers cutting-edge, new technology that may be slightly out of reach as a way to give our patrons a chance to try out technology before buying it, and remain informed. We are also better able to stay up on technology that way, and assist the public in a non-biased way. Unlike a retail store, we have nothing to sell, so we can offer advice and support on a variety of devices. We look at this as an extension of community literacy—technological literacy, which is extremely important in the world we live in.

Although developers are currently working on games and other applications for the Oculus Rift, this is truly an example of the library helping to introduce the concept of wearable technology as much as it is supporting any one particular device at any given moment. There is no doubt that the "gee whiz" factor is one of the things getting users into the library to check out these new devices, but there is also at the same time an acclimatization and normalization process that the library is helping to facilitate as well. Again, I don't believe it's a coincidence that such companies as Google have reached out to librarians as potential guides for its Google Glass device; in this respect I would not be surprised to see other technology firms attempt to leverage the library community in a similar capacity for their own devices in the future.

ADDITIONAL LIBRARY CASE STUDY

University of South Florida

Send in the Drones . . . But Only If the Feds Allow

Exactly what constitutes "wearable technology" is a subject for debate, especially for such a relative new and fluid concept as wearable tech. For example, what about devices that are not necessarily worn but nevertheless augment or extend the sensory capabilities of the user/operator, such as binoculars, microscopes, telescopes . . . or even remote-controlled drones? Even if the technology is not wearable tech per se, the recent proliferation of inexpensive unmanned aerial vehicles—or drones—presents a host of opportunities for commercial, recreational, and education application, as well as myriad potential challenges as their increased presence brings issues of surveillance and privacy toward the forefront of the public consciousness.

While I must admit that drones are somewhat beyond the scope of this book at the time of its writing, I would feel remiss if I didn't share that one of the student projects for our university's loanable Google Glass program is to explore the feasibility of controlling a drone with Glass (some enterprising souls have already combined the Oculus Rift VR headset with the camera controls on a drone in order to provide an immersive "First Person Flying" experience). This leads one to the interesting question: if you could operate a drone with another piece of wearable technology, does the drone become wearable tech by associa-

A quadcopter drone. © Thinkstock

tion or proxy? While you perhaps ponder what the future may bring in this regard as both wearable and remote sensory technologies become ever more ubiquitous, let us mention that the University of South Florida (USF) announced over this past summer that it would begin circulating drones as part of its loanable equipment program.

Alas, it is still waiting on permission from the Federal Aviation Administration to proceed with this one-of-a-kind library loan (for more information, see Mark Schreiner, "What Happened to USF's Drones?" *WUSF News*, September 8, 2014, http://wusfnews.wusf.usf.edu/), but assuming that the legal issues will eventually be addressed programmatically, does this mean that librarians will be offering flight lessons as part of its basic information literacy repertoire? "One of the things many libraries have struggled with," explains Bill Garrison, the dean of USF Libraries, "is how do you become a real part of the campus and not be viewed as a book warehouse. I find it very exciting that we are able to do this, and I think the students will appreciate it" (Megan Garber, "At This School, You Can Check Out Drones Like Library Books," *Atlantic*, June 23, 2014, http://www.theatlantic.com/). That is, if the feds ever clear them for takeoff!

5

STEP-BY-STEP LIBRARY PROJECTS FOR WEARABLE TECHNOLOGY

Now that we have explored the history and current scope of wearables, and taken a few sneak peeks at where the field of wearable tech is going over the next few years (more about this in chapter 7, "Future Trends"), how can you bring some of this cutting-edge technology back into the library for your patrons to experience for themselves? In this chapter you will find several projects with step-by-step instructions that will enable you to highlight the latest in wearable technology and incorporate it into any library setting.

Some of these projects are somewhat technical; others are very do-it-yourself and would be an excellent weekend afternoon activity in your library Makerspace. Due to the rapidly developing market for wearable technology, I have tried to make the instructions as generic as possible, so that you may adapt a project for your existing wearable-technology devices. Don't be afraid to experiment! For example, for the projects involving Google Glass, consider downloading some of the relevant apps (such as Word Lens) to a smartphone or tablet instead. For projects involving QR codes and NFC tags, you may substitute any wearable-tech devices or smartphone with the built-in ability to read either of these delivery mechanisms.

Practical considerations that apply to specific projects will be enumerated under their respective project heading. For more general tips, tricks, and guidelines for loaning and supporting wearable technology in a library setting, please refer to chapter 6, "Tips and Tricks."

HOW TO CIRCULATE WEARABLE TECHNOLOGY IN YOUR LIBRARY

The simplest way to introduce wearable technology into your library, of course, is to loan it from your circulation desk. But how does one best accomplish this? Do you simply attach some barcodes to your devices, put them in the catalog, and let patrons reserve them and check them out as they please? Or do you prefer a more mediated approach to circulating wearables, vetting potential users in order to manage their expectations appropriately and ensure that your patrons have a positive and productive experience when borrowing a strange new gadget from the library? Either approach has its merits, and in this project we will show you how to enable both forms of circulation for your library community.

Instituting a Project Proposal Loan Program

While it is possible simply to loan wearable technology through your library as you would any other kind of device or computer—that is, the patron reserves the device, checks it out at the desk, and returns it at the appointed time, with no additional mediation by the library staff—you may also want to consider loaning these kinds of items on a project proposal basis, especially at the outset of your wearable-technology program when the cost of the new technology is high and the total amount of devices is limited. There are other good reasons for loaning wearable tech in this manner as well:

1. The library may evaluate proposals on their merit, to produce the most potential benefit for the loan period desired and weed out loan requests that do not do anything innovative or interesting with the device.
2. Projects can be scheduled in advance throughout the year, ensuring that library patrons will not have to rely on chance in order to get access to loanable wearable-technology devices when it is most useful for them to have it.
3. Well-defined project proposals will often have a finished end product that can be shared with the library or institution and

used to showcase or promote your library's wearable-technology program.
4. Since each project proposal outlines the intended purpose and use of wearable technology, it is much easier to focus one's support efforts in order to help master any initial learning or development curves and ensure that the patrons get the most out of their loan period.

Short-Term versus Long-Term Projects

One of the most important questions to ask your project proposal applicant is for how long they would like to borrow your wearable-technology device. For Google Glass, a good default loan period might be two weeks, as it gives patrons using such a device for the first time a chance to familiarize themselves with its operation, ascend the learning curve for expert use and simple customization or development, and still manage to incorporate Glass into their teaching or research in such a way as to produce some tangible end product in less than two weeks. Two weeks also builds in a small cushion of direct support time in case there are any actual technical issues requiring direct assistance or escalation to the vendor's support.

Best Practices for Soliciting and Evaluating Project Proposals

An excellent way to solicit project proposals for your wearable technology is to establish and promote a regular cycle for applications, especially in academic libraries, where you can set your deadlines based on the semester schedule.

Here is an example of a sample application for a wearable-technology loan project proposal:

- Proposer's e-mail address:
- Proposer's full name:
- Semester or term in which applying for device:
- Duration:
- Other duration (if applicable):
- A detailed description of the proposed use of device, including activities, app usage, and assessment:

Showcasing and Promoting Wearable-Technology Projects

One consideration for loaning wearable technology at your library is whether or not you will require patrons or groups that borrow the device to share their experiences, using it a condition for loan. This will ultimately depend on whether you wish to circulate your wearable technology on a more casual, first-come, first-served basis, or whether you prefer to loan the devices out through a project proposal process.

For example, as part of our Bass Glass Project we ask our faculty, student, and staff applicants to be willing to share some tangible final product with our advisory group so we can post or link to it on our WordPress website; we also ask patrons who have had success in incorporating our Google Glass devices in their research and instruction to consider joining us at various library and technology events and other showcases so they can share what they've learned and inspire future such collaborations on campus.

In addition, during Yale's 2014 Commencement activities we asked for two graduating volunteers from our Student Technology Collaborative who would be willing to wear two of our Glass devices during Commencement Week in order to capture the experience of graduating from Yale University—one student as an undergraduate, and the other as a graduate student in a master's program. The resulting footage, which the two students agreed to share with us, was edited into a short video that our group posted to YouTube (Yale ITS, "Yale 2014 Commencement: Graduating Glass," August 18, 2014, https://www.youtube.com/) and can now be shared via various Yale communications outlets in order to promote the university and the Student Technology Collaborative, and showcase our creative use of new technologies as an ongoing commitment to experimentation and innovation at our institution.

How to Circulate Wearable Technology to Your Patrons

Practical Considerations

Before you can begin circulating wearable technology to library patrons, there are several practical concerns. We will address general practical concerns that are common to all forms of wearable technology first and then address those concerns specific to Google Glass subsequently.

Circulating Wearable Tech

The established best practice for loaning your devices is to do so through your library circulation system. Create item records for each device, defining the loan period, renewal policies (if allowed), and fines/fees for late returns or missing/lost materials. Whether or not you should create additional item records for important accessories—such as chargers or cases—depends in part on whether or not your integrated library system (ILS) is able to handle pop-up messages, as instead of checking out each component separately it may simply suffice for the library staff to verify that all circulating components are included with the device upon check out and return.

Fines, Fees, and Replacement Costs

Just as library users accept responsibility for overdue fines and replacement fees for any library material they borrow and fail to return, return late, or return in damaged or unusable condition, they must also assume the same responsibilities for borrowed library equipment. Since the due dates and replacement fees for lost, damaged, or destroyed electronic items is usually much greater than that of the normal amounts for library books, it is standard practice to alert patrons to these increased fees during the reservation or checkout process. Some libraries also include additional notifications that are attached to the container provided with the circulating device as an extra reminder.

To Insure or Not to Insure?

As the replacement fees for wearable technology can easily total over $1,000 (e.g., the Glass Explorer edition of Google Glass currently sells for $1,500 before tax), some libraries strongly recommend or even require that users sign up for property insurance to cover the replacement cost of the item.

Best Practices for Returning Wearable-Tech Loans

Upon return of a wearable-tech device, library staff should be trained in the proper deletion of any remaining personal images or data in the device's memory or storage. This is especially important with items that sync to an individual's online accounts—for example, Google Glass is designed to pair with one's Google account. For many devices, the best practice for ensuring patron privacy and online security would be to perform a factory reset, which restores the device to its initial settings and allows the next patron to pair with the device with his or her own online identity without encountering any login errors or conflicts caused by certain onboard default applications being associated with a previous user's account.

HOW TO USE GOOGLE GLASS AS AN ALTERNATIVE TO TRADITIONAL INFO/REFERENCE

It happens all too often at library public service desks: a patron will come to your most visible service point in search of help, only to find that the person behind the desk is distracted by whatever it is on his or her own computer workstation monitor. Even when library staff members are assisting patrons with their query with the utmost diligence and courtesy, the formality of the desk and the abstraction of the need to look up information online can foster a sense of separation and aloofness.

Libraries have experimented with various methods of addressing this problem—sometimes with monitors that can swivel or additional displays that can be used to draw the patron into the public service interaction, but sometimes by eliminating the barriers of the desk entirely through "roving reference" or other unconventional public service models. Perhaps the most compelling potential use for Google Glass and other forms of wearable technology is the ability for library staff members to interact with patrons without having to hide behind a desktop computer in order to access the information they need.

Librarian, Heal Thyself

In fact, the health-care industry is already experimenting with this functionality. Although the ability to quickly and efficiently access a patient's medical records, potential symptoms, and possible drug interactions had made the introduction of mobile technology, handheld devices, and tablets a boon to physicians, the fact that doctors now spend the majority of their visits looking at computer screens and not interacting with

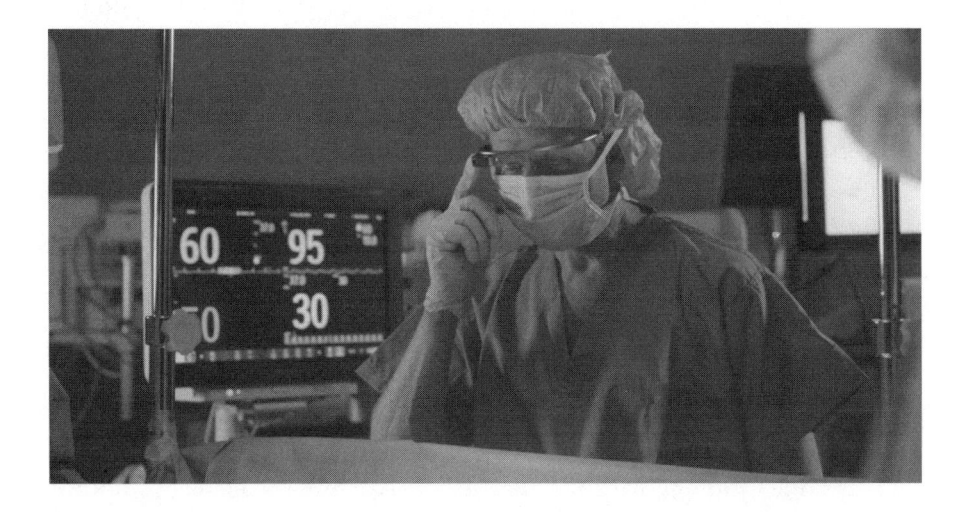

A physician in the operating room uses Google Glass. *Source:* "Experience the Future of Wearable Technology: Philips Healthcare," Philips, accessed April 20, 2015, http://www.healthcare.philips.com/.

their patients has been a major cause for complaint in patient satisfaction. Some hospitals have attempted to address this issue by incorporating Google Glass into the examination room. By using wearable technology to access vital patient information and other necessary information as needed, doctors can maintain eye contact with their patients and use the onboard camera and image-recognition applications in order to enhance their clinical diagnostic abilities during the visit, even calling in other physicians for consultation using Glass's teleconferencing functionality through Google Hangouts. After a highly successful limited trial, the Beth Israel Deaconess Medical Center in Boston now uses Glass throughout its entire emergency department, and other hospitals are quickly following suit (Callum Borchers, "Google Glass Embraced at Beth Israel Deaconess," *Boston Globe*, April 9, 2014, http://www.bostonglobe.com/).

From the ER to the Help Desk

Configuring Google Glass for use in a hospital setting, where personal medical information must be carefully guarded accordingly to strict federal guidelines, has required significant modification of the wearable-technology device used by medical IT professions, but a similar real-time roving reference presence can be achieved in a library setting with much less initial investment and development. Does your library already have a mobile presence online? Then you can use Glass and other forms of wearable technology to easily access this layer for timely retrieval of relevant information. Does your library use QR codes anywhere in the building or elsewhere on campus? Incorporating Google Glass into your roving reference program is one way to finally maximize the potential of this oft-neglected and much-maligned shortcut to online information.

The following project will show you how to use Google Glass to enhance your public service presence. It will require some staff investment time on your part as you train them to use the Glass interface so they are not fumbling with the device while simultaneously attempting to meet your library patrons' information needs, but the potential for deploying your public service staff members where they can be the most effective greatly outweighs the time and effort required to make this possible. Also, the adoption and successful use of wearable technology by library staff in such a highly visible manner raises the public profile of your library and helps project an image of a relevant, technologically savvy, and forward-thinking institution to library patrons, visitors, and other important stakeholders such as alumni and donors.

Using QR Codes and NFC Tags in the Library

Pity the poor QR code. Invented in 1994 to facilitate the tracking of vehicle component parts in factories, the QR code—short for "quick response code"—or two-dimensional barcode (the term QR code is actually a trademark), while finding myriad commercial application in such fields as shipping tracking, logistics, product inventory, and other situations where scanning a barcode through various stages of a supply chain is technically feasible, has been slow to catch on with consumer use, despite some interesting and even outlandish attempts to incorporate them into the mainstream (such as QR codes on cemetery headstones!). In the library world, QR codes have been met with either indifference or outright ridicule as being a waste of time, money, and effort—see, for example, the amusing YouTube video "The QR Code

Minute with JP and PC" (PC Sweeney, January 28, 2013, https://www.youtube.com/).

NFC—or near field communication—tags have suffered a similar fate in the library world. Although they enjoy practical application in shipping and supply-chain logistics, as well as growing commercial success in the gaming industry (see the popular video-game-cum-collectible-action-figure phenomenon Skylanders, as well as Nintendo's recent Amiibo line of NFC-powered figurines for use with its WiiU games Super Smash Brothers and Mario Kart 8), NFC tags have been slow to catch on in libraries as well.

Some good-natured ribbing aside, one of the interesting potential applications of wearable technology is to make it easier to utilize both the QR code and the NFC tag. Google Glass, for example, is able to read and process QR codes, and most models of smartwatch currently on the market are able to read NFC tags. Of course, both QR codes and NFC tags can be processed by many existing smartphones, usually by downloading an application. Here we will look at library projects that will allow you to take advantage of QR codes and NFC tags to create location-based information for your library's virtual presence, adding augmented-reality serendipity to your stacks and pushing out other useful information to your patron in order to maximize both its visibility and its usefulness (see also in chapter 7, "Future Trends," for some information about iBeacons and BluuBeam, which utilize a third way of broadcasting info to your library patrons).

For a great set of best practices for the creation, placement, and assessment of QR codes, see Andrew Wilson's excellent "QR codes in the Library: Are They Worth the Effort? Analysis of a QR code Pilot Project" (in the *Journal of Access Services* 9, no. 3 [2012]: 1–17). I will summarize Andrew's six steps here:

1. Identify your online content.
2. Make sure your online content is appropriate and optimized for mobile devices.
3. Identify and test the QR code location.
4. Create and link the QR code.
5. Take necessary steps to allow tracking and assessment of usage.
6. Embed the QR code into the signage, and post in the desired location(s).

Glass Explorer and developer Jonathan Warner has created a third-party scanning application called QR Lens (http://okaysass.com/posts/14-08-04-qrlens-google-glass-qr-scanner) that can be installed via the sideloading process, as mentioned earlier in the book. Once installed, you can activate the QR Lens application by saying, "Okay Glass," and then "recognize this" while looking at the barcode through the Glass viewfinder—the QR Lens app will then read the QR code and redirect you to the embedded URL. The value of this project is not just in its relative simplicity and cost-effectiveness but also in the fact that you are able to support multiple handheld, mobile, and wearable-tech platforms with the same project. For example, any QR codes that are readable via Google Glass can also be easily scanned and read by any smartphone. To take this project just one small step further, we will now combine QR codes with another augmented-reality tool—near field communication (or NFC) tags—so that we can add support for other forms of wearable technology, including smartphones and smartwatches.

You can buy NFC tag stickers from a number of online vendors, such as Go To Tags (http://www.buynfctags.com/). Stickers tend to cost between about eighty cents and a dollar per unit for blank stickers, and roughly double that amount if you wish to have something preprinted on them—such as your library's name. Once you have these stickers you will need to encode them. While this is something that any NFC tag vendor will also do for you for an additional charge, you can easily do it yourself by using any NFC-enabled device, such as a smartphone.

Overview of NFC Tag-Writing Applications

There are in fact many different apps for the Android operating that will enable you to encode and edit your smartphone tags: see NFC Tagwriter, NFC Tools, or NFC Writer in the Google Play Store, just as a few suggestions. Support for NFC in Apple devices, including iPhones, iPads, and other Apple handhelds, is a more complicated problem. Although Apple has included NFC functionality in the hardware for the iPhone 6 for its own proprietary and restricted use, the latest version of iOS (as of the time of this writing, iOS 8) does not support the ability to read or write NFC tags, although its upcoming Apple Watch—to be released in early 2015—does have NFC capabilities. Obviously the practical application of NFC, which similarly to QR codes languished following their initial inception and struggled to catch on with mainstream public use, is becoming much more apparent and attractive in a world where wearable technology is trending toward ubiquity, so one would imagine (or at least hope!), that the iPhone 6 and future releases of the iOS operating system will follow suit in time.

NFC tags can contain not only embedded URLs but other encoded information as well, including fairly specific instructions to mobile devices to launch certain applications, but for the purpose of this project we will simply encode each tag to point the wearable device or smartphone that taps it to point to the finding aid or other mobile library web information that we've already embedded in the previous QR code project. Now we should also adjust our QR code signage to include a space for the NFC tag sticker and the legend—"Scan the QR code or tap your device here for more information."

Suggested Content for QR Codes and NFC Tags

Try to anticipate what information would be of maximum utility if it were pushed out to patrons at various physical locations in your library. For example, place research guides adjacent to the relevant portions of the stacks, a list of upcoming programming next to a function room, or even links to databases or readers' advisory applications at key locations in your library. One simple yet extremely useful QR code link is to place QR codes outside of study rooms that can be reserved online—scanning the barcode takes the library patron directly to the online reservation application, which shows them both availability and gives them the ability to reserve the room themselves on the spot.

Using QR Codes and NFC Tags for a Library Scavenger Hunt

Now, what if you ignored all of the best practices for the placement of QR codes and NFC tags in your library, so that instead of making them easy to locate and scan, you go out of your way to hide them throughout your library building and stacks or in your neighborhood or college campus? What you've created for your library patrons is the perfect recipe for a scavenger hunt! Whereas most traditional scavenger hunts involve handing out a list of hidden goals to your patrons and letting them check them off as they go, relying on the honor system as they do so, an augmented-reality library scavenger hunt could utilize QR codes and NFC tags in order to assist with tabulating scores and keeping your library scavengers honest.

Anne Burke, Adam Rogers, and Adrienne Lai from the Instruction Supports Services staff at the North Carolina State University Libraries designed a mobile scavenger hunt to help familiarize new students with the library ("Instruction Support Services: NCSU Libraries Mobile Scavenger Hunt," NCSU Libraries, last updated June 13, 2014, http://www.lib.ncsu.edu/). Their scavenger hunt used a combination of iPod Touches linked to a shared Evernote account in order to collect each team's results in a central online location that could be analyzed quickly and efficiently by the librarians who were charged with "keeping score." Adding QR codes or NFC tags to such a scavenger hunt would allow players to check in automatically, reducing the amount of overhead involved in administering such a program and allowing the game to run continuously in an asynchronous fashion.

HOW TO INITIATE A WEARABLE-TECHNOLOGY TRAINING PROGRAM FOR LIBRARY STAFF

Organizing Technology "Petting Zoos"

What fun is adding new technology like Google Glass to your library collection if you don't give library staff a hands-on opportunity to use it and play with it as well? In this section we will show you how to organize and run a successful "petting zoo" for your library staff. Not only do these kinds of live interactive demonstrations provide an introduction to wearable technology for staff, but also they can also serve as a powerful promotional tool for administrators and other key stakeholders. Petting zoos can also be expanded to include library patrons as well as faculty and student groups—just be mindful to keep your group manageable, as wearable technology is still extremely new and will draw quite a crowd of people who want to see, wear, and experiment with a device such as Glass. With successful preparation, however, petting zoo events are a great way to show off the capabilities of wearable technology to a wide audience; even with the inevitable glitch here or there, every

Google Glass petting zoo I've run has generated a great deal of enthusiasm and library staff are always appreciative for the opportunity.

Space Considerations

The first thing you need to do in order to organize a wearable-technology petting zoo is to consider your venue. Ideally, you'd like to have a space where people can gather but are free to move about somewhat, like a meeting or seminar room or a function room in your library. While it might seem like a good idea to hold a petting zoo event in a central location, these kinds of activities can be loud and somewhat disruptive, and depending on whom you have invited you may or may not end up with additional curious onlookers who'd also like to get a peek at Google Glass. Be sure that the room either can get a cell phone signal or at least has reliable wi-fi access, as the Google Glass device will need one of the two in order to function optimally! If the room has a large display with HDMI input, that would be extremely useful as well, as you can use Glass's ability to screencast what it sees as a way to demonstrate its capabilities to other audience members while they wait for their turn to play with the device.

Batteries Not Included

The next consideration is battery life. As I have already mentioned before, one of Google Glass's chief limitations at the moment is its somewhat anemic battery life, which places a practical limit on any potential petting zoo activity you might want to organize. Glass is meant to conserve power by shifting into "sleep" mode whenever it is feasible—in a live demonstration setting, however, the device will be in constant use, so be prepared for no more than an hour and a half of continuous operation before your Glass's onboard battery is exhausted. (As another consideration, the device tends to run hot when it is being used nonstop. Not only can this be a nuisance to the person wearing the device, but also it is also possible for the device to overheat, which will cause limited functionality until it has had time to cool down.) So be sure not to schedule your petting zoo for any longer than an hour and a half at most. This is something I learned the hard way when I organized my first petting zoo for Yale Library staff: I had advertised a two-hour session and had to turn away several disappointed staff members who

Google's Chromecast device. Photo by Erica Joy, Flickr.

applications of varying levels of stability and reliability. In the fall of 2014 Chromecast included the ability to stream a "mirror" of one's mobile display, which used in conjunction with Google Glass's screencasting functionality through the MyGlass app can make the process of broadcasting your Glass display even easier than before, although bear in mind that this feature is still only experimental in Chromecast and you will need to purchase a Chromecast device and a display with HDMI inputs in order to display content in this manner.

Here are the step-by-step instructions for displaying Google Glass content using Chromecast:

1. Plug your Chromecast device into the HDMI port of the monitor or television on which you wish to display your Google Glass content.
2. Open the Chromecast application on your mobile device. Select the "Cast Screen" option and confirm on the next page.
3. Go to the MyGlass app on your mobile device and select the "screencast" option.

4. Activate your Google Glass device—the contents of the onboard display should now be screencasting to your mobile device and Chromecasting to your monitor or television.

Semper E-Paratus

Finally, in order to maximize the potential interaction during your petting zoo, you want to make sure you have a repertoire of "go-to" applications and short activities that show off some salient features of wearable technology while allowing your zoo-goers to have fun while learning about the new device. Obviously one of the things that people will want to do with Google Glass is to have their picture taken while wearing the device; rather than discourage this activity, you should instead be prepared for it and bring a mirror to the petting zoo so that participants can take their Glass "selfies" using the device itself and not simply have someone take a picture of them using their own phones. This is one of the reasons Google Glass has full-length mirrors close on hand for your first Glass "fitting." As I asked my Glass guide in New York City who assisted me with getting started with my device, taking a picture of yourself wearing the device is inevitably the first thing that people want to do when they first put them on (in other words, we are all Glassholes at heart). Other attendees may want to take short videos. Fortunately the default setting for recording video on Glass is ten seconds, so it is very easy to do so; moreover, while the wearer of the device is recording their video, others will be able to see what they're seeing on the screencast.

Google Hangouts—Just Add Glass

If you have a friend or colleague who also uses Google Glass and a reliable enough wi-fi connection or cell phone signal, you could get ambitious and attempt to show off the video conference capabilities using Google Hangouts by inviting your remote friend to join your demonstration. The interesting thing about using Glass in a Google Hangout is that instead of having a webcam pointing at you, the other participants in the Hangout will see what you're seeing while wearing the device. With two devices in a Hangout with one another, this remote telepresence will be an extremely interesting and unusual two-way experience.

Obama participates in a Google Hangout (sans Glass, unfortunately). Official White House photo by Pete Souza.

This kind of telepresence is of course of great interest to medical professionals and other disciplines where bringing in another expert's opinion via remote sensing could be invaluable—imagine what public service staff members could do if they were following the first-perspective video of a library patron while attempting to navigate the stacks, or of a staff member in training. (Note: If you happen to have two or more of your own Glass devices on hand you may be tempted to experiment with this functionality as well. A word of caution, however: because of the way that Google Glass tethers with a mobile device, you can currently only be paired with one Glass at a time. This means that anything requiring a Google account, such as a Hangout or other online device-to-device communication, will require two separate mobile devices with two separate Google accounts for pairing.)

Sharing Glass with Social Media

Linking your Glass with social media can make your petting zoo interactive with your larger online circle of friends and fans in real time as well. Google Glass automatically syncs itself with the associated Google+

account, but there are official Glassware apps that support posting pictures, videos, and status updates directly to Facebook and Twitter as well. If your library has a strong social media presence, setting up Glass so that it can post to your news feeds while the petting zoo is taking place might be a fun way to highlight the event and draw your library staff or other attendees into enhancing your social media presence. Just be sure to let attendees to your petting zoo know that any pictures and video may be posted online during the hands-on demonstration beforehand so there are no misunderstandings.

Show Us Your Glassware

Aside from these simpler functions, you can also show off some of the more "gee whiz" capabilities of the device by installing the right onboard applications for your petting zoo. Google's current offering of official Glassware has several apps that I'm particularly fond of showcasing in front of a large audience, which I will enumerate here in turn:

1. Strava Running. Obviously you won't be taking your petting zoo attendees on a jog, but this fitness app designed by Strava (who also makes a cycling Glassware app) is a great way to show off the usefulness of Google Glass when used in conjunction with a heads-up display showing direction, speed, and other metrics during one's run. You can also break the ice somewhat by making your petting zoo attendees run around in circles in your demonstration room, which is always a good time.
2. Minigames. It's a fun fact that when Google first launched Glass, its developers were dead-set on excluding any games from the device—which to me is an almost mind-bogglingly inexplicable blind spot on their part in trying to encourage more people to warm to this form of wearable technology. At some point in the development cycle, however, they relented, releasing a small package of minigames that includes tennis, skeet shooting, and a 360-degree puzzle matching game that truly highlights the immersive virtual potential of wearable technology. Which of these games will prove to be the Solitaire or Minesweeper of the Google Glass operating system? Have your petting zoo attendees play a couple of a games, and let them be the judge!

3. Word Lens. While there are possibly more ambitious Glassware apps available from Google, the Word Lens application if demonstrated correctly will always elicit the most oohs and aahs from your petting zoo attendees, so I highly recommend that you try showing it off to a larger audience. Word Lens provides real-time translation from several major European languages into English, or vice versa, simply by looking at the text you'd like to translate. For the purpose of a seamless demonstration, you want to prepare the texts you're interested in translating in advance—make sure they are easy for both the device to recognize and for the audience to read if following along on the screencast. For the best results, use actual printed words and not handwriting on a blackboard or whiteboard, and set up several examples around the room so that various attendees can try translating using Word Lens when it's their turn to play with the device. When this application works correctly, it's like magic, so definitely invest the time and effort into setting this up!

HOW TO CREATE FIRST-PERSON VIDEOS USING GOPRO CAMERAS

The Wearable-tech Revolution Is Already Here

The GoPro camera was invented by Nick Woodman, a surfer cum entrepreneur who was frustrated by his attempts to capture his surfing adventures on film via traditional means (i.e., hiring a photographer) and was inspired while on a trip to Indonesia to design a rugged and relatively cheap wearable camera that could literally be taken anywhere. GoPro cameras have been on the market for over ten years now, during which time they have evolved from 35 mm cameras to fully digital cameras capable of recording in HD video.

When we think about wearable technology, the GoPro is often overlooked these days by flashier new devices and concepts, such as Google Glass or smartwatches, but this obscures the fact that the GoPro is by far the most successful form of modern wearable tech both in terms of sales and in terms of adoption by the mainstream public. This makes adding one or more GoPro cameras to your library's collection of circu-

An example of the Word Lens app in use on a smartphone. *Source:* Word Lens demo, Quest Visual, Inc.

lating wearable technology very feasible, as the devices are comparatively cheap, resistant to breakage or water damage, and easy for even a technology neophyte to pick up and use. I've half jokingly referred to the GoPro as a "poor man's Google Glass"—this is not to disparage Glass for its expensive price tag or GoPro for being some kind of Google Glass knockoff but is a basic acknowledgment that people who are enamored first and foremost with Glass's ability to record first-person point of view (POV) video might want to consider picking up and playing with a GoPro camera instead.

Consider the Alternatives

In fact, this is exactly what our Bass Glass Project steering committee does when we are evaluating new project proposals from our faculty, students, and staff. If we determine that someone is basically only interested in Google Glass for the purposes of recording video footage, we steer them to borrowing one of our GoPro cameras instead; if you are considering adding Google Glass to your library's collection of wearable technology, you should definitely consider adding one or more GoPro cameras as well for the very same reason. While Glass does an adequate job of capturing first-person video, the GoPro is vastly superior to Google Glass in this functionality for several reasons:

1. Ability to record in HD video up to 1080p 60fps, or even 3-D video if using a multicam setup; Glass only records in 720p.
2. Longer battery life. While recording continuously, a GoPro3+ camera can last between two and three hours depending on settings and whether or not wi-fi is enabled, whereas the battery life on Google Glass is less than half of that.
3. Storage space. GoPro cameras save video to MicroSD cards, which allow you up to 128 gigabytes or more of storage memory. Glass is currently limited to 12 gigabytes of onboard flash storage.
4. Durability. The GoPro camera is designed for active use and can be worn while performing a variety of tasks, including sports and other recreational activities. It is shock resistant and water resistant down to a depth of 197 feet. Google Glass on the other hand is difficult to wear during athletic activities, as there is currently no means by which wearers can securely mount the device to their head, and the device is still extremely susceptible to moisture.
5. Cheaper. Even the current highest-end models of the GoPro camera can retail for as low as $300, whereas the price tag for Glass is still $1,500. Consider the needs of your patrons, and make your purchasing decisions accordingly.

One of the more creative first-person POV videos I've seen using a GoPro camera here at Yale was during the 2012 commencement, when our Office of Public Affairs and Communications mounted a GoPro camera to Handsome Dan, our beloved bulldog mascot who traditionally makes an appearance during the graduation festivities. You can see the resulting video here: "The 'Dan Cam': A Dog's-Eye View of Commencement 2012," *Yale News,* May 2012, http://news.yale.edu/.

Library Walkthroughs Made Easy

While you may not want to strap a GoPro camera to a dog and turn it loose in your stacks, there are several different interesting ways you could incorporate first-person video into your library's instruction and programming. Here we will demonstrate how to use a GoPro camera or similar video-capture device in order to create library walkthroughs and other first-person POV tutorials for your library patrons and library staff.

One thing to keep in mind when making video recordings in your library is always to respect the privacy of your patrons—even if someone is not the focus of your video, you should make sure that you obtain the permission of everyone who appears in your videos before publishing them online, or if you are unable to obtain permission, that you edit the footage to remove anyone who does not wish to be filmed (or anyone whom you were not able to contact about permissions). For this reason it is often useful to create your first-person POV videos during low-volume, low-traffic times of the day in your library. Also consider filming just before the library opens, for example, or just after the library closes.

Remember to Keep It Simple

Another consideration for creating instructional videos is to keep them short. A recent analysis performed by comScore of the top ten watched videos on YouTube showed that the average length of these videos was 4.4 minutes ("ComScore Releases January 2014 U.S. Online Video Rankings," comScore, February 21, 2014, http://www.comscore.com/); an additional study by Wistia showed an additional correlation between video length and user engagement, demonstrating that for online videos of approximately four to five minutes in length only 60 percent of viewers will watch the entire video, whereas over 80 percent of viewers will remain engaged for videos that are thirty seconds or fewer in length (Ben Ruedlinger, "Does Length Matter?" Wistia, May 7, 2012, http://wistia.com/).

Brevity, is seems, is not merely the soul of wit but also the key to creating watchable online video content, so when you are creating first-person footage always try to keep your content short and sweet. Be sure to storyboard your videos in advance and write a basic script of what you want to say. By all means you want the video to appear natural and not forced, contrived, or overly polished, but bear in mind that every second you spend rambling on the camera represents at the very least one less viewer who is going to watch your video from start to finish.

Consider therefore breaking up longer video tutorials into smaller chunks. Thirty seconds may not seem like a lot of time, but it is possible to provide a brief overview for one short topic in that interval; that should be your goal.

Choosing a Subject for Your Video

The simplest subject matter for a first-person POV walkthrough is demonstrating how to find a book. You can record yourself making your way from your library's entrance to the nearest workstation connected to your online card catalog, look up a book by title or author, write down the call number of the item, and then move toward your library stacks in the proper direction—this in turn is an excellent segue into a video tutorial about your library's stacks layout, highlighting the major eccentricities of how your material is shelved in your library. Do you have a famous individual or noteworthy author associated with your library? It can be a fun video project to show how to find one of their books in your collection.

For example, when Umberto Eco came to Yale University to speak in January 2014, he mentioned that his original inspiration for the labyrinthine library in the medieval library featured in his novel *The Name of the Rose* was based on his experience of getting lost in the mezzanine of Yale's Sterling Memorial Library. To commemorate both Professor Eco's visit and his creative inspiration, I decided to create a first-person video showing how I navigated one of those same mezzanine floors in order to find one of his own books on the shelf, which I posted online to YouTube (Tom Bruno, "Finding Umberto Eco in the SML Stacks #ThroughGlass," January 27, 2014, https://www.youtube.com/; although I had used Google Glass to record this video, the principle for recording these kinds of POV walkthroughs is exactly the same. Note that I tried to keep the video to just over four minutes in length, although I couldn't help but ramble a little, even after several takes!).

Tutorials for Library Patrons and Staff

One of the more frustrating aspects of creating tutorials for library patrons or staff is that most library activities are almost always some kind of blend between physical and virtual tasks, making it difficult to capture the process from start to finish using some kind of screen-capturing application such as Camtasia or Captivate. Take, for example, using a library copier/scanner to scan, save, and send a file to yourself; in order to properly document how to use this device, you would need to show the requisite component physical tasks (e.g., where to insert your USB drive, how to place the materials on the scanning bed properly, and how to start the equipment's scanning interface) and then show the tasks that the patron or staff member need to perform while using the equipment's operating system as well (e.g., how to change the scanning settings, how to process an image after scanning, and how to save the image to a USB drive, send it via e-mail, or upload it to another online service).

These "blended" tutorials, however, are perfect for a first-person walkthrough video, using a head-mounted camera such as either GoPro or Google Glass. In this section we will show you how to create these first-person tutorials and how to easily embed them both online on your library website and physically by means of QR codes and NFC tags.

1. Select an appropriate activity to document with a first-person tutorial. The best activities for this kind of POV video documentation is an activity that is either entirely physical (for example, how to shelve a book) or a blend of the physical and the virtual (like the above example of how to scan a document using a library copier/scanner). For activities that are performed entirely online, you should consider using some kind of screen-capturing application—such as Camtasia, Adobe Captivate, or one of the myriad free alternatives—or documenting the activity via static screenshots and pasting them into an online slide deck. The reasons for this are simple: even when using a high-resolution camera, recording a video of a computer screen will always be harder for your intended audience to read than a born-digital screen capture itself.

2. Determine the appropriate length of the POV video tutorial. I have talked about the ideal length of an online video elsewhere in this book. Let the "two-minute rule" be your guide for recording any kind of first-person tutorial. If the task is sufficiently long or complicated that you would need more than two minutes in order to properly or thoroughly document it, consider storyboarding

the activity so that you can break it down into component chunks that could be recorded separately and posted as step-by-step activities. For example, going back to our scanning documentation, you could create a series of shorter videos describing how to access the physical interface of the copier/scanner device; best practices in placing materials on the scanning bed and best practices for the proper care and handling of library materials when copying or scanning (these are old examples, and I violate my own rule of thumb about keeping the videos short, but here is a series of scanning care and handling videos for library staff that follow the concept of breaking the activity down into thematic components: "S&D Guidelines and Information for Library Staff," Scan & Deliver, accessed April 20, 2015, http://isites.harvard.edu/); how to process images after scanning using the onboard image-processing software; and then a final short video on how to save, send, or upload your scanned files.
3. Record your video using the first-person video-capture method of your choosing—be it a GoPro camera, Google Glass, or another form of camera-equipped wearable technology that is capable of recording POV video. Remember that every second counts, so even if you think you're pretty good about speaking extemporaneously, consider writing a script or at the very least a series of bullet points that you can use to rehearse with and keep yourself on track.
4. Edit your video as appropriate. There are myriad applications available for editing video footage—from expensive high-end paid video-editing software to free online applications. For the purpose of creating tutorial videos such as these, I would argue that functionality is more important than form, and getting something created, useable, and available online for your library patrons and staff is much better than getting it "perfect," but bear in mind that if you are posting these videos to a website that is searchable to the public online and your institution has "look and feel" guidelines for online videos, make sure that you are conforming to these rules! Since I almost always upload my videos to YouTube, I am fond of using the online editing tools that are available there, which allow you to perform a variety of simple postproduction tasks such as cutting and pasting footage, adding

titles and credits, overlaying a soundtrack, and myriad other digital effects.
5. Create a QR code or NFC tag pointing to your video online. Please see the project about using QR codes (or the subsequent section about NFC tags) for detailed instructions for tips, tricks, and best practices.
6. Place your QR code or NFC tag in an appropriate location—that is, adjacent to the space or equipment for which you have designed your video tutorial. The best part about physically embedding a tutorial in this manner is that you are able to offer help to the library patron or staff member in the most helpful place possible, in the form of a first-person video.

HOW TO ADD REAL-TIME TRANSLATION SERVICES USING GOOGLE GLASS

One of the most memorable things from Douglas Adams's rollicking and bizarre science fiction series *The Hitchhiker's Guide to the Galaxy* is the miraculous Babel Fish, a tiny little creature that the denizens of the galaxy place in their ear in order to receive real-time instantaneous translation of any language they hear. While the idea of automatic translation is a common theme in sci-fi—witness the Universal Translators in *Star Trek*, the translation circuits of the TARDIS in *Doctor Who*, or the existence of neurotic polyglot protocol droids in the *Star Wars* movie franchise—the Babel Fish proved to be a powerful enough inspiration to programmers and software developers that one of the very first online translators, created by AltaVista in 1997, was actually called the Babel Fish. Since then mobile and wearable technology has continued to evolve in the quest for ever more seamless translations capabilities, whether it is automatically detecting the language of a website and translating it into the user's native language, or taking spoken or written words from the real world and attempting to transcribed them and translate them on the spot.

Word Lens and Real-Time Signage

The Word Lens application was developed by former videogame developers Otavio Good and John DeWeese in 2010. It is an augmented-reality program that uses optical character recognition (or OCR) in order to recognize writing and quickly translate it into one of several other supported languages. Although Word Lens was a very successful paid mobile application for iOS and Android devices, the owning company Quest Visual was recently acquired by Google, which had already added Word Lens to its stable of Glassware applications and intended to incorporate the application more broadly into its Google Translator services. Currently the Word Lens application supports the following translation schemes:

English to Spanish
English to French
English to Italian
English to German
English to Portuguese
English to Russian

It is unclear if and when other languages—including those utilizing non-Roman alphabets and scripts—will be supported.

One of the more interesting aspects of Word Lens is that it does not require an Internet connection in order to translate text. All of the application's OCR and translation capabilities are already built into the application's software, meaning that Word Lens can render a translation almost as quickly as it can recognize and process the imaged text. This means that you are able to place translatable signage in areas with limited cellular data or wi-fi connectivity. Also, although we are featuring using Word Lens with Google Glass for this project, because it is freely available for smartphones as well you can instruct patrons to download the application and use it to translate your signage on their own device. However, for the sheer magic of the experience nothing quite compares to seeing real-time translation happening while actually wearing Glass and watching the words change in the heads-up display!

How to Use Word Lens with Google Glass

1. Install the Word Lens application in the official Google Glassware store (please note: although the application, once installed, does not need external data in order to work, this step will require network connectivity), either using the onboard operating system on the Glass device or via the MyGlass application on your tethered mobile device or computer.
2. When Word Lens has been installed on your Google Glass, activate the application by saying, "Okay Glass, translate this."
3. When Word Lens launches, be sure to hold your head steady while looking at the signage you wish to have translated for you. The translation will appear superimposed over the OCRed text in the sign.
4. Tapping the Glass device while the application is running will give you the various supported language translation options available to you.

Here are some important considerations for getting the best possible translation results from the Word Lens application:

- Make sure the text you wish to translate is printed in a large and relatively common font, as Word Lens's onboard OCR capabilities have a hard time recognizing handwriting or unusual fonts.
- Although you don't have to worry about cellular data or wi-fi connectivity, make sure the signage is easy to look at through the Google Glass viewfinder and it is not difficult to hold your position while waiting for the application to OCR the text and render its translation—that is, be sure not to put signs that are in dangerous or high-traffic areas, or areas where it would be awkward for a person to stop and stare for a moment.
- The smaller and simpler the amount of text to be translated, the better the results. While Word Lens can be used on larger text blocks such as handouts or pages from a book, the application tends not to work nearly as well in this context. Also keep in mind that real translation is a science and not an art, which means the simplest texts will result in the best literal translations. Word Lens does not translate according to context or "sense," so be sure that

your signage is written in as plain English as possible and mostly free of colloquialism.

We have already mentioned that Word Lens makes for a dramatic application to show off at a Google Glass petting zoo or other large-scale demonstration, especially if you are able to project the results on a screen as you use the device. Using Google Glass with Word Lens could also make for an interesting twist on a library scavenger hunt, by creating special signs for library users to discover and translate in order to reveal hidden clues or checkpoints in the scavenger hunt competition.

Captioning: Present Accessibility, Future Promise

Another powerful accessibility tool for Google Glass has only recently been added to the official list of supported Glassware app: Captioning, a new application that utilizes both your Glass device and your smartphone microphone in order to stream closed captioning for live speech on the Google Glass display. Developed by the Georgia Institute of Technology, Captioning leverages the existing speech-recognition technology that creates subtitles for YouTube in order to transcribe spoken words in real time. While the results can be highly variable, the Captioning app usually provides enough context for users who are hearing impaired to understand the gist of a conversation and follow along. The researchers at the Georgia Institute of Technology who developed this application are also working on connecting this output to live translation, which would expand Google Glass's translation capabilities into the audio and the visual. In the meantime, while offering Glass as an audio accessibility device is not necessarily a library project per se, it is an excellent way to promote the exploration of adaptive technologies in your library community and demonstrate the practical utility of wearable technology to your patrons, staff members, and other stakeholders.

HOW TO USE WEARABLE TECHNOLOGY AS A PROMOTIONAL TOOL FOR YOUR LIBRARY

Best Practices for Sharing in Social Media

One of the more interesting aspects of wearable technology is its potential integration with social media. Google Glass, for example, is designed to interface with a Google account; not only can it automatically send pictures, videos, and status updates to Google+, but also by loading various Glassware applications you can easily link your device to Facebook, Twitter, and various other social media sharing sites. Google is aware of the impact of social media in helping to build buzz around Glass and uses the #throughglass hashtag as a way to promote content distributed on social networking sites.

Here we will discuss how to leverage these social media capabilities within your own library using wearable technology. Please be advised that some libraries have informal or formal guidelines about posting or sharing on social media sites on behalf of your institution, however, so make sure you touch base with the person responsible for your library's communications to see if there are any rules you need to comply with. For example, my university has guidelines regarding institutional branding for any audiovisual materials created and disseminated online by Yale University faculty, students, and staff.

First-Person Ambassadors of Wearable Tech

A simple way to promote wearable technology at your library is to ask someone to use the device during a special event, such as a reception or party, a concert, or any other large gathering. In the spring of 2014, we loaned two of our Google Glass devices to graduating students so that they could capture moments from their commencement activities from a first-person perspective. One of the students even wore the device on the commuter train down to New York City in order to document picking up her relatives at the airport so they could attend her graduation as well. The resulting edited footage comprised an emotional vignette showing what it's like to graduate from Yale University and will be used not only as an example of successful use of wearable technology at our library but as a powerful promotional tool for the entire university as well.

Other institutions have experimented with turning the first-person perspective around and asking teachers, administrators, or other guests of honor to wear Glass during special events to show what attending such gatherings is like from the vantage point of the podium. This of course requires your dignitaries to be good sports about wearable technology and willing to experiment with the devices in a high-profile public setting, but the potential payoff and resulting positive buzz for your library and your institution can be well worth taking the risk.

Taking Your Wearable Tech on the Road

Another relatively simple venue for showcasing wearable technology in libraries is to send your staff to a conference using wearable tech. Jenny Levine, strategy guide for the American Library Association (ALA), has worn her Google Glass device to several library conferences, including ALA's Midwinter Meeting and Annual Conference. As she mentions in an article in *American Libraries Magazine*, getting used to wearing Glass throughout the conference involved overcoming her own hypersensitivity about using the device in such a public setting:

> At first I had to force myself to wear Glass around the convention center, because it can feel ostentatious—like a neon sign flashing "1%" (the price tag is $1,500) and "Really Geeky Person." But then an interesting thing happened: I started to realize I was much more comfortable wearing Glass in front of strangers than around friends and neighbors. Walking around Philadelphia, I didn't care if the person I just passed on the street mentally called me a "Glasshole" (the most common derogatory term for people who wear Glass). (Jenny Levine, "Between a Google Glass and a Hard Place," *American Libraries Magazine*, February 7, 2014, http://www.americanlibrariesmagazine.org/)

Bringing the Conference Back Home

This kind of project however does not simply serve as a potential promotional tool; because wearable technology makes social sharing so easy to do, devices such as Google Glass could possibly enhance the virtual conference experience for your own library staff or other librarians who might not be able to attend such conferences in person. For example, Glass's seamless integration with Google Hangouts allows for first-person teleconferencing capabilities, making it feasible to send one library staff member into a meeting on behalf of an entire group. This kind of virtual representation, which currently relies on antiquated means of communication such as conference calls and telephone speakers, could be vastly enhanced as wearable technology offers a more natural and organic telepresence for potential virtual conference-goers.

How might venues such as ALA and other library conferences better accommodate this style of representative remote attendance in the future? As a past devotee of the virtual world Second Life, which enjoyed a brief but exhilarating period of interest from librarians during its heyday, I wonder how wearable technology might help us realize the possibilities we began to explore in the context of virtual worlds by blending the online world with the real world.

There are lessons here to be learned for sure: if virtual librarianship floundered and failed because of the clunkiness of the interface and therefore the steep learning curve required to master such a platform, then as advocates for wearable technology in libraries we must be careful to choose devices and applications that do not present similar barriers to adoption and widespread use among both our patrons and our colleagues. Can Google Glass and other forms of wearable technology meet these criteria for usability? Only time will tell.

MAKE YOUR OWN IMMERSIVE VIRTUAL REALITY HEADSET USING GOOGLE CARDBOARD

Perhaps sensing that Oculus Rift was stealing its thunder, at their annual I/O Conference in June 2014, Google recently released Google Cardboard, a do-it-yourself, immersive virtual-reality headset kit made out of cardboard and magnets that turns any Android smartphone into a 3-D viewer. Google Cardboard is the brainchild of David Coz and Damien Henry at the Google Cultural Institute in Paris; they designated the Cardboard prototype using their "20% Time," which is provided to all Google employees in order to foster an environment of innovation, experimentation, and creativity. (The concept of "20% Time" has always

My daughter Andriana tests out Google Cardboard. Photo by author.

had its champions and detractors, and even Google has tempered its own unbridled enthusiasm for the idea itself, but the fact is that carving out this time for staff and allowing them to dedicate it to tinkering with pet projects has borne a disproportionate amount of positive returns for Google—leading to successful products such as Gmail, Google Talk, and AdSense—and is an ideal worth replicating in your own organization in some capacity. If not setting aside an entire day out of each week to encourage your library staff to learn and try new things, try to give them as much creative latitude as your institution will permit.)

Google Cardboard, which delivered a low-cost but high-impact virtual-reality experience, became wildly popular in-house at Google and was quickly spun off as a public project. As such, it makes a perfect project for libraries, as it combines wearable technology with a DIY component that would fit well in any library with a Makerspace or similar hands-on program for patrons. The total cost of the building materials is relatively cheap—between twenty and forty dollars per assembled kit—and Google has released a suite of free apps for Cardboard in its Google Play store so your patrons can play with their Google Cardboard prototypes as soon as they finish building them! As far as Cardboard's relevance to libraries is concerned, all I know is that librarians have shown great interest in doing hands-on demos with Google Cardboard in both academic and public libraries. Here at Yale University we recently held a technology showcase featuring Google Cardboard, and many public libraries with makerspaces see Cardboard as a cheap and fun way to let their patrons experience virtual reality hands-on with a DIY project.

Here is what you'll need in order to host your own Google Cardboard project in your library:

- Cardboard for the virtual-reality headset. The Google Cardboard project recommends using an E-Flute, which is a thick and sturdy version of corrugated cardboard. The design files containing the patterns for cutting the cardboard to the correct specifications can be found at "Google Cardboard," https://www.google.com/get/cardboard/.
- Two lenses with a 45 mm focal distance, although on its Cardboard website they say that they use the 22 mm OpenDive Lens Kit from DuroVis.
- One neodymium ring magnet and one ceramic disk magnet. Why magnets? From the Cardboard FAQ: "The magnet is used for clicking inside of demos. When you pull and release the ring, your phone's magnetometer detects changes in the magnetic field."
- Two strips of Velcro and one rubber band.
- One NFC (near field communication) sticker tag, programmed with the URL cardboard://v1.0.0. While the NFC tag is not required, it makes it easier for Google Cardboard to automatically launch its Cardboard-mode applications when you insert your smartphone into the viewer.
- A ruler, glue, scissors, and either an X-Acto knife or a laser cutter.

Note: Depending on how much of a "Maker" component you want here, you can jumpstart the DIY steps of a your own Google Cardboard project by purchasing online kits that come with all of the necessary components. Some of these kits come with the cardboard already precut and ready for assembly, while other kits arrived entirely preassembled. The company Unofficial Cardboard (https://www. unofficialcardboard.com/products) sells pretty much every permutation of the Google Cardboard kit, from fully assembled models to just the bare-bones components with or without the cardboard; so does the San Francisco-based company DodoCase, which actually includes its own selection of virtual-reality applications along with its Google Cardboard clone viewer. So feel free to decide how crafty you'd like this project to be! From personal experience, putting together a precut Google Cardboard kit is easily a project that can take one or two hours, making it a perfect "one-session" option for a library looking for such an activity.

Immersive VR Applications

Once you have assembled your Google Cardboard viewer, you can explore the various apps that Google and other developers have created (i.e., Cardboard will work with other virtual-reality headset apps, with varying levels of compatibility) in the Google Play store. One of the most interesting Cardboard apps available currently is Tuscany Dive, which allows you to take a panoramic walking tour through a villa in the Tuscany region of Italy. There is also a virtual rollercoaster simulator that is guaranteed to make you feel as if you are actually on the ride yourself as you loop the loop.

There are also virtual-reality games such as SpaceTerrorVR, flight simulation apps such as Flight VR Demo, and VR Cinema for Cardboard, which allows you to watch MP4 videos in 3-D. My daughter and I had the opportunity to assemble our own Google Cardboard kit (we purchased ours through DodoCase) and explore most of the aforementioned applications. It's absolutely astonishing that with approximately twenty dollars' worth of cardboard and an ordinary smartphone you can create your own DIY immersive virtual-reality experience, but that's exactly what we were able to do over the space of a rainy Saturday afternoon.

Students of film history may remember when they talk about the first movie audiences and how they actually panicked and tried to get out of the way when they saw the locomotive bearing down on them on the screen. I always read about those reactions with a little bit of amused condescension, but putting on our homemade Google Cardboard I think I actually experienced a little bit of that fear and wonder myself, as did my daughter, who couldn't stop trying to get out of the way of objects as she approached them in her virtual walkthrough of that Tuscany villa. If nothing else, consider doing this project in your library to help share this sense of amazement at the potential of immersive virtual reality, which although only at its inception is poised to have a monumental impact on the way in which we experience digital media.

6

TIPS AND TRICKS

Additional Considerations for Wearable Technology

There are some practical concerns regarding wearable technology that we will now address. While some of these tips and tricks are specifically about Google Glass, many of the themes explored here are universal to the emerging wearable-tech market and can easily be applied to most devices currently available and to those that will enter the consumer marketplace in the next year or so.

MIND YOUR POWER

First, there is the issue of battery life. As mentioned before, Glass is an experimental prototype, and one of its chief shortcomings as such is the fact that its built-in rechargeable battery has a very short life span when the device is in full use—no more than two hours of continuous use will run Glass down from a full charge to empty. While the device is designed to minimize battery drain when not actively being used, many of the tasks for which Glass is ideal are those that use the heads-up display or the camera, both of which use power very quickly. Library users interested in using the device should be aware of this limitation, as they may assume that the item will hold a charge for as long as a smartphone or other electronic accessory, only to find that their ambitious plans for Google Glass have been foiled by the relatively short battery life.

POWER OPTIONS FOR WEARABLE TECH

One would hope that future commercial releases of the device will address this issue, but in the meantime one can augment the battery life by means of an external battery, such as the HyperJuice external battery for Apple iOS and USB devices. Using Glass while attached to one of these power sources could be cumbersome, however, and while Google has not expressly cautioned against the use of third-party charges and batteries with Glass because the item is still a prototype, some additional measure of caution might be warranted.

GOOGLE GLASSING WITH GLASSES

A second issue particular to Google Glass is difficulty of using the device when wearing eyeglasses or other corrective lenses. As Glass is designed to be worn on the face just like a pair of glasses, it fits only awkwardly at best if worn over an existing frame; also, because many of the functions of Google Glass have a biometric component, wearing them atop another pair of glasses can confuse or confound these motion or activity-sensing functionalities. Although to their credit Google has recognized this shortcoming and addressed it by making it possible to combine Glass with custom prescription frames, obviously this is not a solution for being able to make this device usable by a wide variety of library patrons, many of whom may wear corrective lenses.

This is a difficult problem for libraries to remediate, one that can cause additional troubleshooting headaches when attempting to facilitate demonstrations with larger groups, as there is nothing as frustrating as being unable to use an exciting new piece of technology because of accessibility concerns. While this is no means a perfect workaround, being able to mirror Google Glass to a screen or tablet by means of the MyGlass application offers a way for patrons who are otherwise unable to use the device to see what a Glass user "sees" when they are using it. We will discuss how to use this mirroring function in greater detail later in this book, as well as suggest additional projects or activities using this screencast capability.

HOW TO NOT PROMISE THE MOON WITH WEARABLE TECHNOLOGY

Finally the third major issue that may emerge while supporting a circulating Google Glass device is how to manage patron expectations when borrowing and using experimental technology such as Glass. Until very recently, there were only a handful of Glass Explorers (the inaugural group of invitees only numbered eight thousand) using the device in an extended closed beta period. Although the ranks of this program have now been opened by Google, development of applications for Google Glass—otherwise known as Glassware—has proceeded very slowly, with still only a few dozen Glassware apps available for download via the official MyGlass application. The availability of third-party Glassware has been steadily improving as an ever-larger group of application programmers now have development access to the device, but it is still a somewhat cumbersome and dangerous process to "sideload" these unofficial Glassware applications onto a Glass device.

EXPERIMENTAL TECHNOLOGY AND THE LIMITS OF PATRON-DRIVEN DIY

Just as with any other Android device, there is great flexibility and potential for customization, but along with this freedom comes the possibility of being able to "brick" (i.e., render inoperable) one's device. Although do-it-yourself-ers now feel comfortable with rooting their Android phone, with a $1,500 price tag these same DIYers may think twice about attempting to modify their Google Glass device—as will most librarians and their IT departments!

To be fair, Google appears to be making a conscious effort to add more "interesting" official Glassware offerings. While the original Glass development team did not wish to include games, for example, there is now a minigame application included on the MyGlass apps page that features skeet shooting, tennis, and other diversions that may one day become the Minesweeper or Solitaire of wearable technology. Google has also made it easy to pair one's device with any of several popular social media platforms—such as Google+ (naturally), Facebook, and Twitter—and offered additional apps that organically introduce Glass into existing augmented-reality applications for other mobile devices. All of this being said, however, there is a great deal of development work yet to be done in order to realize the full commercial potential of Google Glass, such that patrons may find themselves disappointed when they finally get a chance to use the device only to realize that the applications currently available are limited in scope (unless you play golf, as there are at least two official and several unofficial Glassware apps for improving one's game—never let it be said that software development does not follow the money!).

KEEPING IT REAL

How does one then manage library patrons' expectations of what Google Glass can or cannot do? This is where "petting zoos" and other demonstrations can be of great utility. Many patrons are simply interested in seeing what Google Glass is all about, and events such as this can help satisfy that curiosity, as well as help patrons make informed decisions about how they would use wearable technology such as Glass were they able to borrow it from the library on a subsequent date. We will describe the basics of how to facilitate a wearable-technology petting zoo in the next chapter, but another useful way to help patrons understand how to get the most out of using these devices is to provide short tutorials and other documentation online that is posted to your library website. If you are loaning wearable technology to groups or individuals, consider asking users to share pictures or video from their use with the library, so that other patrons can view these vignettes as potential use cases of their own. Here at Yale we have asked our short- and long-term project loans to agree to provide a tangible final product that we can share in turn with the community.

KNOWING YOUR WEARABLE TECHNOLOGY

Another way in which library staff can help frame patrons' expectations is to know their wearable-technology equipment well enough themselves to provide useful advice as to which device is good for what purpose and to make recommendations appropriately based on this

TIPS AND TRICKS   91

knowledge and experience as sort of a wearable-tech "Readers' Advisory." For example, patrons who are interested in taking first-person videos while performing strenuous physical activity might want to consider using a GoPro or other wearable camera instead of using Google Glass. Other patrons may find the hands-free heads-up display abilities of Glass more useful to their purposes than the same information delivered through a mobile device or tablet, or a smartwatch or FitBit.

In general, the more knowledgeable your library staff is about new technology, the better interpreters they can be of these devices for your library patrons. It is therefore just as important to hold demonstrations and other outreach sessions internally as well as externally. Your goal in offering a loanable wearable-technology program is not to impress yourself, your community, and your peers with being "cutting edge" in your embrace of the Next Big Thing but to provide the most conducive environment to your patrons as they experiment with and explore these new technologies. For all of its flashiness, always remember that technology is only as useful as your library's ability to support it.

TROUBLESHOOTING WEARABLE TECH

"Tom, I think there's a problem with the Google Glass."

These are the words that I have come to dread. Working with a wearable-technology device that is still in its experimental development phase is fun, except when something goes wrong. No sooner had we added our third Google Glass to our Bass Glass Media Equipment program than one of the other partners had contacted me about our second device, which was failing to turn on after many different attempts to reboot and reset it. Did an online update in the Android operating system go wrong? Or was there an issue with the onboard battery? Whatever the case, our Glass was dead in the water, so it fell on my shoulders to contact Glass Support at Google and try to diagnose and troubleshoot the problem. One of the drawbacks of using Glass in an institutional setting is that while your local library IT department might be able to offer some limited support, there is no substitute for working directly with Google if something serious goes wrong. This is not just for the practical reason that Glass Support is much more likely to be able to offer a solution to your problem when you do find yourself in a situation where technical troubleshooting is required, but also since Google Glass is only selling the device to individual Google account holders at this time there will be a point in the support protocol where only the account holder will be able to proceed with the repair or replacement process.

This is something you may want to keep in mind when considering who should be responsible for administering your loanable Google Glass program. If the point of contact is not in a position to be able to make time for contacting Glass Support and walking through the entire troubleshooting triage process when a technical problem does occur, then you may want to consider who might be the most strategic staff member in your organization to serve in such a liaison role and make sure that the Google Glass purchase is made using their Google account. (There is an interesting and amusing upside to being the designated go-between in this manner—after all, it's not every day that you call someone at Google and they already know you by first name because you've discovered a brand-new problem with their shiny new product!)

WHAT'S GOOD FOR THE GLASSHOLE...

Although the above advice is specific to Glass, the general theme here is that the more new and experimental the technology, the more laborious the troubleshooting process will be for any loanable devices in your library's possession. Also, consider what the impact of a broken or current inoperable device would mean to your library's wearable-technology program. I am not going to pretend that every library is fortunate enough to be able to purchase three Google Glass devices as we have at the Bass Library here at Yale, but even with this relative luxury we have crafted a system of short- and long-term loans that depend on there being multiple Glass available at any given time for our faculty, students, and staff to be able to pursue their individual projects. If your library has the wherewithal to purchase a backup device, I would always use this as your best practice; failing that, however, consider having similar wearable-technology devices on hand to fill some of the desired functions as needed—for example, having a GoPro camera available for loan would allow library patrons to at the very least shoot first-person videos if your Google Glass device was currently unavailable. Remember that an important part of managing your patrons' expectations with loaning wearable technology is having a plan of action for when this technology is on the blink or in the shop. This is especially so as your patrons become more familiar with wearable technology and therefore have had time to form their own expectations of what their library should be able to offer them in terms of availability and support.

WEARABLE TECHNOLOGY AND PRIVACY ISSUES: PATRON PRIVACY AND PUBLIC PRIVACY

Wearable Technology and Legal Issues

It is clear that there are still myriad privacy and legal issues that remain to be settled with wearable technology. As Google Glass and other "wearables" become more ubiquitous over time, society will no doubt come to some sort of consensus about what constitutes reasonable use of wearable technology and what doesn't. For example, in little more than a decade, cell phones have evolved from being disruptive novelties that were always considered rude or ill mannered to use in public regardless of the context or situation to being items that virtually everyone owns and uses on a regular basis (although we still may disagree on whether or not it's okay to take a call in a restaurant or check your smartphone in a crowded movie theater). It stands to reason therefore that wearable technology will follow a similar evolutionary path in our hearts and minds from objects of derision and awkward conspicuous consumption to things that we couldn't imagine living without.

The legal dimensions of wearable technology will likely work themselves out as well over the next five to ten years. Already law enforcement is struggling to make sense of these new devices—for instance, is it legal to drive while wearing Google Glass?—and the courts will no doubt help clarify the rules of engagement in defining what constitutes lawful or unlawful use of wearable tech and how to strike a balance between the public and the private that items such as Glass seem to blur at the moment.

HIPAA and Wearable Tech

In the meantime, however, there is one respect in which the law is absolutely clear regarding Google Glass and other forms of wearable technology: the Health Insurance Portability and Accountability Act of 1995 (or HIPAA) mandates that health-care providers and medical clinicians operating in the United States ensure the privacy and security of patient health-care information according to strict standards of compliance. Google Glass and other forms of wearable technology are not considered to be "HIPAA-compliant" and therefore must be modified significantly before such devices can be used in a health-care setting.

In the case of Glass, all of the onboard Google Services built into the hardware and software must be removed or disabled, and all of the apps loaded onto the device must comply with HIPAA's standards regarding protected health information (PHI). This is similar to how other mobile devices such as iPads, older handheld computers such as PalmPilots, and smartphones have been incorporated into hospitals and other medical practices, and in fact there are already technology companies, such as Pristine, that specialize in providing HIPAA-compliant versions of Google Glass commercially available to health-care workers (Aditi Pai, "At Least Four Startups Are Now Focused on Google Glass Apps for Doctors," MobiHealthNews, April 17, 2014, http://mobihealthnews.com/).

What does this mean for your library's wearable-technology program, however? It does put the onus on you to identify any projects involving your loanable devices that could potentially run afoul of HIPAA. For example, in our current round of proposals for using Google Glass here at Yale, we had a couple of faculty members from our medical school who expressed interest in incorporating Glass into the patient interview process and other aspects of medical triage. However interesting these proposals seemed, we were nevertheless obliged to let the faculty know that our devices were not HIPAA compliant and therefore unable to be loaned out in this capacity, although we will be working with our med school's IT department to see if it might be interested in adding a version of Google Glass that does comply with HIPAA for future such project proposals.

The Social Mores of Wearable Technology

Just as the proliferation of mobile phones in the 1990s introduced a cultural conversation about what constitutes acceptable and unacceptable use of personal communications technology in public—a conversation that has only been exacerbated by the introduction of smartphones and the always-on, always-sharing social media these devices enable—wearable technology has not only upped the ante yet again but also brought new focus to issues of privacy, conspicuous consumption, and the intersection of technology with the social dimensions of race, gender, and class. Google Glass in particular has seemed to provoke the lion's share of the tension surrounding wearable technology, with several high-profile incidents involving people being accosted or even attacked while wearing the device out in public.

When Glassholes (Are) Attack(ed)

Social media consultant Sarah Slocum was wearing Google Glass at a popular dive bar in San Francisco in February 2014 when she was confronted by other patrons who were concerned that Slocum was recording them without their consent. This is a fairly common concern about Glass, so much so that the first question many people ask someone who is wearing Google Glass is whether or not they're currently recording them. Although Slocum made it clear that she was not taking any pictures or recording any video while wearing the device, the altercation quickly turned ugly, at which point fearing for her own safety she did begin recording and captured a ten-second video clip that was uploaded to the Internet and shared widely (Sarah Slocum, "Assaulted and Robbed at Molotov Bar on Haight St. for Wearing Google Glass," YouTube, February 23, 2014, https://www.youtube.com/).

In April 2014, *Business Insider* reporter Kyle Russell was covering a story in downtown San Francisco when a passerby snatched his pair of Google Glass from his face, smashed the device, and then fled the scene:

> A colleague and I had just finished covering a march in protest of a Google employee who had recently evicted several tenants after buying and moving into a home in the area.

After more than an hour spent working on the story in a coffee shop, I arranged my laptop, camera, and notes in my backpack. Mindlessly, I put on Google Glass instead of squeezing it in with the rest of my things. (In retrospect, I can see how that might not have been the best idea.)

The aforementioned colleague and I were on our way to the 16th Street BART station—I'll note that I wasn't using any device at the time—when a person put their hand on my face and yelled, "Glass!" In an instant the person was sprinting away, Google Glass in hand. (Kyle Russell, "I Was Assaulted for Wearing Google Glass in the Wrong Part of San Francisco," *Business Insider*, April 13, 2014, http://www.businessinsider.com/)

Google Glass as Looking Glass

There's actually a lot going on here beyond privacy and simple wearable-technology etiquette. Both of these incidents took place in San Francisco, where Google and the technology sector's prosperity has exposed deep class divisions as well as other tensions. "Here in the San Francisco Bay Area," writes *Salon* columnist Andrew Leonard. "Glass has a huge P.R. problem. Glass is a walking contradiction: A status symbol that many people (the majority?) consider fundamentally uncool. And for both good reasons and bad, Glass has become the symbolic silicon-embodiment of tech-economy-driven gentrification. In a politically charged environment, choosing to wear Google Glass is equivalent to choosing sides" (Andrew Leonard, "The Google Glass Day of Judgment," *Salon*, April 15, 2014, http://www.salon.com/).

Nevertheless, the larger point is that the idea of Google Glass is proving to be just as disruptive, if not more so, as the reality of wearable technology's current capabilities. Until devices such as Glass become more ubiquitous, the notion of "wearing the future on your face" will always seem to be a declaration of sorts, full of symbolism both intentional and unintentional on the wearer's part. Increasingly mindful of Google Glass's social footprint as more and more devices entered the mainstream and not too long after Sarah Slocum was accosted for wearing Glass, Google published an official list of "Dos and Don'ts" for its Glass Explorers ("Glass: Explorers," Google, accessed April 22, 2015, https://sites.google.com/).

Do "explore the world around you," Google exhorts its users; on the other hand, don't "be creepy or rude (aka a 'Glasshole')." That Google recognizes the pejorative slang term "Glasshole" in its own documentation is telling, for it shows that they are aware of the negativity that has surrounded the device so far in the public imagination and are relying therefore on their users to serve as ambassadors for the new technology. What is the role of the library in such a fluid and politically charged context? I would argue that librarians have an opportunity to showcase wearable technology in a nonthreatening environment that emphasizes exploration over exploitation and to introduce the concept of wearable technology to the broadest possible audience without an overriding concern for the bottom line.

THE LIBRARIAN AS TECHNOLOGY EVANGELIST

Google itself seems to understand the special role that libraries now play as intermediaries between new technologies and the public. After several years' conspicuous absence from the library conference circuit, Google returned to the American Library Association's Midwinter Meeting in Philadelphia in January 2014, sponsoring an evening reception featuring library Glass Explorers with the ALA Office for Information Technology Policy and offering live demonstrations of Google Glass for librarians on the floor of the Pennsylvania Convention Center floor ("Try Out Google Glass at the 2014 ALA Midwinter Meeting," ALA News, January 22, 2014, http://www.ala.org/).

While it is uncertain whether Google will continue to pursue a deeper partnership with libraries, the fact that wearable technology will soon become as pervasive as tablets and smartphones will mean that at the very least library staff will need to be able to troubleshoot at the basic interactions between these new forms of accessing library content at the very least. But just as libraries must negotiate an ever more blurred line between technology officially supported by the institution and other devices and applications with which library users will ask for help in using (whether or not supporting these devices is part of the library's stated "job"), librarians need to anticipate a new service paradigm in which their users will be wearing the future of libraries on their faces as well.

Some librarians have already suggested taking an aggressive stand against wearable technology and banning Google Glass from the library on the grounds that they represent a threat to patron privacy, but just as initial library bans on cell phones and digital photography yielded to more measured and nuanced approaches that allowed users to leverage new technology to enhance their use of the library, so too will libraries eventually find a point of equilibrium between the pitfalls and the possibilities afforded by wearable technology.

7

FUTURE TRENDS

What's on the Horizon for Wearable Technology?

OCULUS RIFT AND OTHER 3-D IMMERSIVE SIMULATIONS

In March of 2014, social media giant Facebook shocked the gaming world by announcing that it had acquired the Oculus VR company at a price of over two billion dollars. Oculus, whose prototype "Rift" viewer promised gamers a wearable three-dimensional headset display, was the brainchild of Palmer Luckey, who was fascinated by the prospect of immersive simulation technology and had created several iterations of a head-mounted displays using his own time and money. These experiments, which he documented on MTBS3D (Meant to be Seen 3-D), an online forum for virtual-reality enthusiasts, eventually formed the basis of a Kickstarter campaign that caught the attention of several influential software developers and other members of the gaming community.

The Oculus Rift, still in development, has released two developer's kits so that programmers could begin to experiment with the new device on their own and integrate the Rift into their current projects in development—most notably, John Carmack, the cofounder of Id Software, has promised that the next version of its extraordinarily successful game franchise Doom will be fully compatible with Oculus Rift. Founder of Mojang software and creator of Minecraft Markus Persson (aka "Notch") initially said that he would make the popular Minecraft game compatible with Oculus Rift as well, but Notch subsequently withdrew this promise upon hearing about Facebook's purchase of the Oculus VR company. With Microsoft's even more recent acquisition of Mojang and Minecraft, however, it remains to be seen whether this decision will be reconsidered. In the meantime, as Minecraft has always been relatively easy for third-party developers to tinker with on their own, there is already an unofficial "Minecrift" modification that allows players to experience the Minecraft gaming platform using Oculus Rift.

OCULUS RIFT—NOT JUST FOR GAMING

Museums and other cultural institutions have also been experimenting with using Rift as an immersive reality tool. At the Dutch Rijksmuseum, Europeana has created an Oculus Rift walkthrough of a virtual museum, which they've named the Museum of the Future, containing real works of art on display ("Museum of the Future," Oculus VR, accessed April 22, 2015, https://share.oculusvr.com/). And individual developers are already busy coding their own first-person simulations of such things as the pyramid of ancient Egypt and the iconic spaceship the Millennium Falcon from the *Star Wars* movies. The truly immersive virtual-reality experience has always been something of a "Holy Grail" for videogame and technology enthusiasts, which has made the recent developmental leaps by Luckey's Oculus VR company all the more exciting.

Although many observers decried the company's acquisition by Facebook as a betrayal to the indie developer community, this move can also be interpreted as signifying mainstream interest and confidence in the idea that 3-D immersive technology holds tangible promise for consumers' development and use. Surely such a display has the potential to radically reshape our relationship to gaming, but will these changes translate into the broader spectrum of wearable technology as well? The entertainment industry, which has long struggled with creating 3-D movies that are more than just gimmicks (not to mention 3-D television displays in the home, which have languished even after many attempts at selling the devices to a larger mainstream audience), is already trying to figure out how to incorporate the Oculus Rift into its content.

Meanwhile, some educational institutions and libraries have begun to explore the Oculus Rift as well. For example, the Arapahoe Library District in Colorado was one of the first public libraries to acquire a first-generation development kit following Oculus VR's successful Kickstarter campaign, which it made available to its users to try out at the library.

THE NEXT BEST THING TO BEING THERE

One of the more interesting applications of the Rift display to higher education has been via a third-party startup company. In 2008, the website YourCollege360.com began offering virtual campus tours to prospective college students, assembling photo and video-based walk-throughs for over a thousand campuses around the world; now known as YouVisit, the company actively partners with many of these colleges and universities to create promotional content for recruitment purposes. In 2013, YouVisit began experimenting with the Oculus Rift developer's kit in order to create immersive panoramic college tours that admissions officers can bring with them to high school college admission fairs. This program, while still in a pilot phase, is already proving to be very popular and may in the near future change the entire nature of the time-honored tradition of prospective undergraduate students physically visiting college campuses before making a decision on which school to go to (Julian Chokkattu, "Universities Look to Oculus Rift to Lure Students to Campus," TechCrunch, June 30, 2014, http://techcrunch.com/).

The potential of virtual-reality tourism has not been lost on the travel industry either: just in September 2014, the Marriott Hotel Group unveiled its "Teleporter" booths, which utilizes the Oculus Rift and a clever combination of odors and physical effects to simulate travel to exotic locations around the world, including Hawaii or downtown London (India Sturgis, "Explore Hawaii's Beaches without Leaving the City!" *Daily Mail,* September 19, 2014, http://www.dailymail.co.uk/). It is indeed curious how quickly the Oculus Rift has gone from being a dream project in someone's garage to a borderline mainstream phenomenon—in less time, in fact, than Google Glass has been in its closed "Glass Explorers" beta period.

THE SPECTRUM OF WEARABLE TECHNOLOGY: FROM INVISIBLE TO IMMERSIVE

Does this mean that the Rift is destined to overtake and possibly displace Glass in the not-so-distant future? Well, yes and no. While Oculus Rift certainly has the backing of the gaming and entertainment communities powering its current development cycles, the fact that the Rift is fundamentally an immersive experience places it on the opposite end of the wearable-technology spectrum as devices such as Google Glass. Imagine that Oculus Rift and Glass inhabit a continuum of wearables, with the Rift representing immersive simulation and virtual reality and Google Glass and similar devices representing augmented reality. The goals of these two forms of technology are similar but fundamentally parallel in nature. Whereas Oculus Rift wants to make the real world all but disappear when you put on their headset, Google Glass's ultimate goal is to blend virtual reality and its attendant metadata seamlessly into the real world.

Already however there are companies that are attempting to bridge the divide between augmented and virtual realities. In January 2015, Microsoft introduced its "HoloLens" 3-D augmented-reality viewer, a wearable headset that projects holographic images into the viewer's field of vision. Unlike Google Glass, which creates a small heads-up display in the corner of one's eye, the Microsoft's HoloLens is designed to superimpose images and data onto real-world objects in a dynamic, immersive layer of augmented reality (for a demonstration of the HoloLens in action, see the following video: "Microsoft's HoloLens Live Demonstration," YouTube, January 21, 2015, https://www.youtube.com/).

Both forms of wearable technology have their place, and both have myriad future potential applications for business, educational, and recreational purposes. For this reason it is important that libraries explore both of these strands of wearable technology and make them as accessible as possible to their constituent users, as these two forms of wearables will become more and more ubiquitous over time and will likely end up being future avenues through which library patrons will discover and experience new library content.

IBEACON AND THE "INTERNET OF THINGS"

In November 2014, the Orlando Public Library in Florida launched location-based services in a partnership with Orlando-based BluuBeam, which uses Apple's iBeacon technology in order to broadcast information to patrons based on their location in the library: "Visitors who download the app get an alert about library offers and events. So, for example, if you're searching the third floor stacks for a Julia Child cookbook, you'll receive a message about the library's Cuisine Corner program that features cooking demos by local chefs" (Satta Sarmah, "The Internet of Things Plan to Make Libraries and Museums Awesomer," Fast Company, January 7, 2015, http://www.fastcompany.com/). Posters throughout the library encourage visitors to download the BluuBeam app, which is available in both the Apple and the Google Play stores; once enabled, the application will receive information broadcast from one of twenty-five BluuBeam transmitters that have been strategically placed throughout the Orlando Public Library system. Over thirty libraries currently use BluuBeam to provide location-based services, with similar companies working with other cultural institutions such as museums as well.

One of the chief advantages of iBeacon over using wi-fi or GPS in order to determine location is that iBeacon can be set up anywhere in your library building—even in places where your wi-fi or cell signals are weak or nonexistent. Because iBeacon uses every mobile device's onboard Bluetooth capability, there is no need to worry whether any given manufacturer will have this functionality enabled or not for a specific device—just download the BluuBeam application, and you're ready to go. Finally, since this location is Bluetooth based, the power consumption required is minimal, which means that you won't frustrate your library patrons by running down their batteries in order for them to take full advantage of your augmented library presence.

This lightweight and low-powered solution is a key ingredient to what technologists are heralding as the "Internet of Things," where one's personal digital experience will be increasingly enhanced by consumer electronics that are designed to interact with our smartphones, smartwatches, and other wearable-tech devices. So even as wearable technology continues to develop and evolve on its own tracks, nonwearable technology will also grow more sophisticated, requiring careful thought, planning, and development.

WHAT ARE THE SIGNPOSTS FOR LIBRARIES?

This puts libraries and other institutions in a somewhat awkward position when trying to support wearable technology, similar to the problems librarians experienced when trying to determine how much effort should be dedicated to creating and maintaining their library's mobile online presence. If wearable technology is ultimately something that will serve in a supplemental capacity to existing personal consumer technology such as smartphones, then there may be no practical utility in developing one's own library wearable-technology environment; however, if wearable technology takes off and begins to develop in its own standalone capacity, then we may find ourselves at a similar disadvantage as we did during the mobile technology revolution in trying to keep up with the information and service needs of our library users.

The growing relevance of the Internet of Things, however, suggests that even if wearable technology is something of a "fad," a future in which our library's physical presence will soon converge with its online and virtual iterations is inevitable.

CONCLUSION: THE ONLY WRONG ANSWER IS NOT TO TRY

I'll be completely honest with you—it still remains to be seen whether wearable technology in its present incarnation will be a success in libraries, or whether librarians will come to mock experiments such as Bass Glass and other loanable wearable-tech programs as they now belittle QR codes or virtual worlds such as Second Life. Hindsight is twenty-twenty, however, and even the best tech trend prognosticators are going to get just as many predictions wrong as they are going to get right. Despite all of the mocking, even innovation that fails is a valuable learning experience, and I for one would always rather be the person fumbling and stumbling along the cutting edge and moving librarianship forward with every success or failure rather than hanging back and letting the future happen to libraries instead.

RECOMMENDED READING

One of the most difficult things about writing this book was that there really weren't any other books out there addressing the subject of wearable technology in libraries, so I'm afraid that this reading list is going to be somewhat sparse. To be fair, the field of wearable tech is moving so quickly that any books I do recommend here are in danger of being out of date by the time this book itself goes to press, so your best bet is to follow wearable-technology news and analysis in the following outlets:

    Mashable: http://mashable.com/category/wearables; http://mashable.com/category/wearable-tech
    Techcrunch: http://techcrunch.com/tag/wearable-tech
    Salon: http://www.salon.com/topic/wearable_technology
    Engadget: http://www.engadget.com/topics/wearables
    Digital Trends: http://www.digitaltrends.com/wearables
    Ars Technica: http://arstechnica.com/gadgets
    Guardian: http://www.theguardian.com/technology
    Digital Shift (*Library Journal* and *School Library Journal*): http://www.thedigitalshift.com/

Several industry research reports and white papers have focused on the growing importance of wearable technology in both the educational and consumer sectors:

Accenture. "Racing toward a Complete Digital Lifestyle: Digital Consumers Crave More; Accenture Digital Consumer Tech Survey." 2014. http://www.accenture.com/.

Harrop, Peter, Raghu Das, and Guillaume Chansin. "Wearable Technology 2014–2024: Technologies, Markets, Forecasts." IDTechEx. Last updated September 2014. http://www.idtechex.com/.

New Media Consortium. "NMC Horizon Report." 2013 Higher Education ed. EDUCAUSE Learning Initiative. http://www.nmc.org/.

For a scholarly overview of wearable technology as a whole, I recommend *Garments of Paradise: Wearable Discourse in the Digital Age* by Susan Elizabeth Ryan (Cambridge, MA: MIT Press, 2014). Siva Vaidhyanathan's *Googlization of Everything (and Why We Should Worry)* (Berkeley: University of California Press, 2012) is more about Google and less about wearable technology, but its anticipation of a near future where reality, virtual reality, and augmented reality are inextricably intertwined is food for thought for any library professional who would try to navigate this strange, new blended world. I would of course be terribly remiss if I didn't recommend *Cyborg: Digital Destiny and Human Possibility in the Age of the Wearable Computer* (Toronto: Doubleday Canada, 2001) by Steve Mann, one of the founding members of the Wearable Computing Group at the MIT Media Lab; although the book is now over a decade old, it is a fascinating glimpse into the mind of one of wearable technology's "founding fathers."

INDEX

abacus, as ancient wearable technology, 1
academic libraries, wearable technology in. *See* Claremont University Library; University of South Florida; Yale Bass Glass
American Library Association, 97
Amiibo, 57
Android Wear OS, 10, 25, 27, 28
Apple smart watch, 14
Arapahoe Library District, 43, 101
augmented reality, 102

Babel Fish, 75
battery life, 3, 10, 61, 87
bearable vs. wearable technology, 1
Bluetooth, 3
BluuBeam, 103
Booth, Char, 35, 36
Borg, The, xi, xv
Brecher, Dani, 35
"bricking" a device, 23

cameras, xv, 43
captioning, 78
Casio calculator watch, 1
Chromecast, 63
circulating wearable technology, 35, 37, 38, 39, 50, 51, 52, 53
Claremont University Library, 35, 36
clocks, as ancient wearable technology, 1

Dick Tracy, 14
Disney Infinity, 30
drones, 46

experimentation, how to encourage, 16, 18, 19
eyeglasses and Google Glass, 88

factory reset, 53
fines and fees for circulating wearable technology, 53
Fitbit, 3, 11, 13

Galaxy Gear, 14, 28
gambling, 1
games, 67, 89
geolocation, 30, 32
Georgia Institute of Technology, 78
Glass Explorers Program, xii, xiii, 4, 5, 8
Glassware, xv, xvi, 21, 58, 67
Google (company), 97; "20% time" policy, 16
Google Cardboard, 81, 82
Google Field Trip (application), xvi
Google Glass, xi, xiv, xv, 4, 8, 35, 36, 37, 39, 44, 46, 52, 54, 55, 56, 58, 61, 62, 65, 75, 76, 87, 88, 91, 92, 94
Google Hangouts, 65
Google Now, 29, 30
Google Tango, 32

GoPro camera, 13, 39, 43, 68; vs. Google Glass, 68, 69

health care industry, 54, 94
HIPAA, 39, 94
HoloLens (Microsoft), 9, 102

iBeacon, 32, 103
immersive reality. *See* virtual reality
innovation, fostering, 18, 36
innovation center, library as, xvii, 37, 43
Instructional Technology Group (Yale), xiii, 37
insuring wearable technology, 53
"internet of things", 103, 104
IT support, 16, 17, 36

legal concerns of wearable technology, 93
Levine, Jenny, xix, 80
library scavenger hunt, 59
library staff use, 16, 18

Mann, Steve, 2
MyGlass app, 22

NFC tags, 30, 32, 57, 58, 59, 73; vs. GPS, 32; vs. QR codes, 33, 57
North Carolina State University, 60
NMC Horizon Report, 10

Oculus Rift, 6, 43, 45, 46, 99, 100
Orlando Public Library, 103

Pebble smart watch, 14, 24, 25
personal metrics, 11
"petting zoo" for wearable technology, 38, 44, 60, 61, 78, 90
privacy concerns, 6, 95, 96
promoting wearable technology, 79, 80
public libraries, wearable technology in. *See* Arapahoe Library District; Skokie Public Library

QR codes, xv, 33, 56, 57, 59, 73, 104
QR Lens (application), 58

reference services, 54

Samsung smart watch. *See* Galaxy Gear

Samsung Tizen OS, 25, 27, 28
screencasting, 22, 63
SDK: Glass Developers' Kit, 17, 22; Pebble smart watch, 25
Second Life, 81, 104
showcasing wearable technology projects, 52
"sideloading", 23
Skokie Public Library, 42, 43
Skylanders, 30
smart clothes, 12
smart phones, 4, 10; vs. wearable technology, 12
smart watches, 10, 14, 24, 25
social media, 66, 79
social mores of wearable technology, 3, 6, 93, 95, 97
Star Trek: The Next Generation, xi
Starner, Thad, xi, xix, 2
Strava Cycling (application), xvi
Strava Running (application), 67
student library workers, 17
Student Technology Collaborative (Yale), xiii, 37

tech support and troubleshooting for wearable technology, 41, 91, 92
technological literacy, 44
telepresence, 66, 80
third-party applications, 22, 23
translation, 75, 76
traveling with wearable technology, 40, 80
"try before you buy", 45

University of South Florida, 46, 47

virtual reality, 6, 45, 81, 84, 100, 101; vs. augmented reality, 102

walkthroughs, first-person, 70, 71, 100, 101
Wearable Computing Group, 2, 3
wearable technology glasses, competitors to Google, 5, 9
Word Lens (application), 68, 76

Yale Bass Glass, xii, 37

ABOUT THE AUTHOR

Tom Bruno is the associate director for resource sharing and reserves at the Sterling Memorial and Bass Libraries at Yale University. Previously he was the head of resource sharing at the Widener Library at the Harvard College Library. He received his master's in library and information science from Simmons College and has a BA in ancient Greek and Latin from Boston University. In another life, Tom wanted to be an astronaut, and he eagerly looks forward to filling his first interplanetary interlibrary loan request.

Tom lives in Milford, Connecticut, with his wife, daughter, and baby boy. When he's not writing, working, or riding the train back and forth to New Haven, Tom enjoys fishing, cooking, hiking, and playing Skee-Ball (aka the Greatest Sport of All Time).